# HOME IS WHERE THE HEART IS

*Voices from Calderdale*

Edited by

Ray Rooney, Brian Lewis and Reini Schühle

Everyone has a story
to tell. We find
ways of helping
them tell it.

YORKSHIRE ART CIRCUS
in association with
CONTINUUM
1989

Published by **YORKSHIRE ART CIRCUS**
13/15 Sagar Street, Castleford, West Yorkshire, WF10 1AG

CONTINUUM
33 Ravenstone Drive, Greetland, Halifax, HX4 8DU

© Yorkshire Art Circus & Continuum
© Cover Design: Wayne Clarida and Brian Lewis
© Photographs: the owners and Continuum
© Commissioned photographs: Stephen McClarence and Gill Cliff
Typeset by Print Assist, Castleford
Printed by FM Reprographics, Ravensthorpe, Yorkshire


**Editorial Team**
Ian Clayton, Carole Kettle, Ros Howell, Odette Johansen
Margaret Edwards, Rachel Adam, Rachel Van Riel, Olive Fowler


**ISBN 0 947780 47 5**

Yorkshire Art Circus is a unique book publisher. We link our books with performances and exhibitions and offer workshops for the first time writer.
Yorkshire Art Circus projects have successfully toured Community Centres, colleges, galleries, clubs, galas and Art Centres. In all our work we bring new artists to new audiences.

For details of our programme of performances, exhibitions, conferences and workshops send for our brochure and book list at the address above.

**We would like to thank the following people and organisations for the use of photographs:**

Calderdale Museum Service
Elland Historical Society
Calderdale Housing Department


We would like to thank Trevor Moore of the Greater Elland Historical Society for the reproduction of photographs.

# CONTENTS

**We would like to thank the following people who have contributed to this book:**

Farzana Ali
George Atkinson
Dorothy Bailey
J.W. Bakes
E. Bakes
Walter Barker
Joan Beeby
Eric Berry
Sylvia Bintcliffe
Fred Borne
Claire Butler
Mary Bradbury
Christine Brook
Paula Broadbent
Andrew Bugler
Iris Burbury
John Chatterton
B.Connelly
Stephen Cullen
Margaret Cape
Doreen Carroll
Hilda Clegg
Margaret Clay
Eddie Clutterbuck
Mollie Clutterbuck
Michelle Collins
Sylvia Cookson
Mrs Crowther
Thomas Crowther
Patricia Crossley
Kevin Dolan
Geraldine Doody
June Furey
Brian Fairclough
Jeannette Gabbitass
Gene Gibbs
Basil Gibson
Barbara Green
Brian Gregan
Mrs Harker
Catherine Hanley
Mary Hansen
Raymond Hanner
Jill Harrison
Mark Harrison
Jeannie Heptonstall
Jean Hirst
Sharon Hooley

Mrs Hodgkinson
Saddagat Hussain
Debbie Harrington
Ruth Harrington
Anne Hellewell
Kevin Hayes
Ros Howell
Phyllis Hill
Marion Hill
Sally Hill
Barbara Hood
Nan Kavanagh
Chris Kenny
Bernadette Kendell
Hilda Kershaw
Mrs Keogh
Penny James
Susan Johnson
C. Johnson
Maurice Jagger
Bernard Jessop
Odette Johansen
Imran Khan
Caroline Kirby
Rachel Lewis
Joan Langfield
Anthony Lannigan
Tony Leighton
Miss Lumb
Mr Lomas
Mr McKeating
Mrs McKeating
Phyllis Mitchell
Julie Milnes
Helen Moran
Patricia McNulty
Zahida Mushtaq
Toby Mak
Yasmin Maqbool
Mrs Nellis
Russell Noble
Mark Norbury
John Oates
Marjorie Oates
Malcolm Ogden
Lynn Okulus
Lorna Overend
Winifred Page

Alice Pettit
Barbara Pickles
Judith Priestley
Sandra Pollentyne
Michael Quinlan
Nicholas Parrot
Andrew Pilgrim
Mrs Ramsden
Kath Rice
Mr Reape
Joan Regan
Annie Richardson
Kathleen Richardson
Albert Rinder
Rachel Roberts
Simon Robinson
Tony Stoker
Mrs Sanderson
Mrs Spencer
Fred Skves
Charlene Stanton
Shirley Stead
J.T.Sullivan
Fiona Smith
Mrs Smithies
Malcolm Stooking
Mrs Stowell
Richard Simonet
Mary Taylor
Maureen Thornton
Mrs Tiffany
Lillian Travis
Gloria Walker
Amy Ward
H. Wardle
Martina Weitsch
Marie Wharvell
Judith Webster
Ronald Williams
Mary Whiteley
Ms Wilson
Keith White
A.S. Womersley
Janet Wanklyn
Robert Wanklyn
Rachel Whiteley

# INTRODUCTION

*'When you start remembering, it topples through'*

*Home Is Where The Heart Is* originally started off as a book about council houses in Calderdale. It quickly went beyond the brick and mortar to look at the wider issues. What happened was that the contributors took over, broadening the theme into all forms of housing. The resulting book has actually become strengthened in its original intention. It is still firmly centred on council housing but it provides a clearer context. The bare skeleton of statistics and sociological reports on housing is given flesh and blood by the people at the receiving end of the current housing policies. They voice their very personal views and feelings, their resignation or hope, their setbacks and aspirations.

The book is organised in three sections: "Homes Fit For Heroes" looks at the house as part of the community; "Heroes Fitted Into Homes?" concentrates on the mechanisms of housing development, especially the role of the decision makers and"Heroes Fit Out Homes" looks at the house as an expression of the individual and what people do to turn their house into a home.

"Homes Fit For Heroes" was the slogan coined at the end of the First World War in response to the appalling shortage of decent housing for working class people. Its historic context meant that originally the equal right of unsung heroines was not publicly acknowledged.

In most people's minds "Homes Fit For Heroes" seems to encompass the housing policies especially of the post war period. Garden cities, pre-fabs, high-rise flats, living machines, sprawling faceless estates and small, people-orientated infill developments are all interpretations over the years by politicians, planners and administrators of what constitutes desirable housing. The underlying philosophy of public housing provision as a social obligation and commitment was safeguarded by successive governments.

Until fairly recently council and private ownership were seen as complementary in meeting society's housing demands. The present major changes in housing policy point to an erosion of council involvement. In the end we will be left with two main alternatives — private ownership or private tenancy. The virtual standstill on council house building, the removal of subsidies for comprehensive repair programmes, the selling of council houses and the depletion of existing stock have made it difficult for the great-grandchildren of the heroes and heroines of 1918 to rent good council property.

*Home Is Where The Heart Is* provides a snapshot of life in Calderdale, focussing on all aspects of housing which the 150 or so people who contributed to the book were prepared to talk or write about. We are grateful for their contributions.

*And we will build Jerusalem*
*in England's green and pleasant land*

William Blake

# HOMES FIT FOR HEROES

*Making Communities*

## Mother sang harmony, I sang melody

☐ Caring about the neighbours as much as you care for your own house is what constitutes a good neighbourhood. You can be as friendly and as nice as pie, but if you move into a nice area and paint your house black or play music all night you won't get on. Likewise if you spend all your time caring for your house and garden and you have little time for Mr Jones next door, then you're ruining the neighbourhood. It's like everything else — you need a balance.

☐ We were always singing and when I think of those songs now, tears come to my eyes. Mother sang harmony, I sang melody. Gracie Fields' songs bring back memories.

Looking back from today people might say we were being nosey but actually we were being caring. Some houses would, but in our house you never gossiped. Mother taught me a lot. If she wanted to make a point she would call me to her with, "Now I've got something to say." She would continue, "People with families should never talk about other people's families because they never know what will happen." She meant girls getting pregnant.

When that happened, of course, they talked about it for a time but although one or two didn't get married, most did.

☐ Our house was the biggest in an L-shaped block of four cottages built in the year 1662. As there were nine of us in the family it was the only house in the village with enough bedrooms. Each house had its own outside tub lav and, although it was a bit inconvenient in bad weather, I can't help thinking that they must have been more hygienic than having a toilet inside the house.

We lived there for ten years. I was only five years old when we first moved in but I still have vivid memories of the house and the neighbours, most especially the couple who lived in the corner. Mr Speke was a postman, and at some time in their lives he and his wife had owned a shop of some kind. That must have been a long time ago — nobody seemed to know where they had come from or what sort of business it had been. The Spekes' lav was in a little yard at the back of their house, which added to the mystery surrounding Mrs Speke. The only time she opened her front door was when she wanted one of us to run an errand for her. Always it would be the exact amount of money wrapped inside a note for the shopkeeper, and we were always rewarded in the same way. On our return she would take us into the house, and for me, that was a short journey into wonderland! The floor was covered in neat stacks of cardboard boxes interspersed with equally neat piles of newspapers, rising to the ceiling like stalagmites. She would lead me through to the fireplace and sit me down while she went back amongst the boxes where I could hear the rattle of a sweet jar. There were always eight boiled sweets in the packets she gave me, and a reminder that two were for me and one each for my brothers and sisters.

I don't know what the grown-ups thought about Mrs Speke but I thought she was special. She had long, wavy hair and a face which only showed kindness and serenity. When the village was preparing to celebrate King George's Silver Jubilee Mrs Speke gave my mum seven enamelled pin brooches, each one different but each one with a royal motif. They were beautiful. We wore them with pride, and now every royal celebration reminds me of the lovely lady in the corner house.

☐ Sixty years ago, women had so much hard work to do. There were no labour saving devices, it was blackleading iron fireplaces, raking coals out, preparing big set-pot boilers for washing and boiling clothes. In each house there were long wooden tables, scrubbed white, to scrub shirts on. For all that our mothers still had time to take us out into the fields to make daisy chains. My job, at about eight years old, was to operate the wringing machine. On washing day there was a big rope stretched out from house to house for the washing. When the coal man came the street rushed out to get the clothes props lifted up.

☐ I was fostered by my aunt. She had a sweet shop on Haugh Shaw Road but it closed in 1940. My aunt was a single lady, and she was crippled, but she also took in another niece rather than let her go to the Bluecoats. I used to kick the irons off my clogs so that I could go to Tommy Atkins' cobbler shop to watch him working. He used to sit there with a mouth full of nails. As a young child I thought he spat them into the clogs to fix the irons.

## You don't easily move from a neighbour like that

☐ One of the reasons why neighbourliness breaks down is because no one wanders off aimlessly with a child in a pram any more. Nowadays a lot of women go off in cars, get to where they are going and then return. This means that they do not say things like, "It is a lovely day," or "How's the baby?" to a woman they accidentally meet hanging out washing a little farther down the street.

☐ Neighbourliness is not a thing of the past in our street. It still goes on and

Hebden Bridge 1989

Stephen McClarence

*New Street, Elland c. 1900*

develops with the years. Take my next door neighbour, for instance. I moved into the odd thirteen over twenty years ago. I'd scarcely been there a month when early one morning, about six o'clock, my baby started to come. This coincided with the water pipes in my neighbour's roof bursting. Well, the baby was not delivered until about twelve o'clock. For all that time water was pouring into my neighbour's ceiling, threatening to bring it down, yet she was forbidding the plumber to turn off the water. Three of us shared the same main and she reckoned that with the baby coming I would need plenty of water. You don't easily move from a neighbour like that.

☐   Your closest friends were the women whose kitchens faced yours over the other side of the backs. Most of our lives revolved around kitchens. That is where the toy tub was and where a mess could be made without too much trouble. It was the community who looked after the children. If you were going upstairs to do a bit of vacuuming then you shouted to a neighbour and she kept an eye on your child. Later in the day you would do the same for her. If a child wanted a drink he or she didn't necessarily go home but went to the nearest door. My husband reckons that a well worn track goes from our door to the biscuits.

☐   When I got to the street I was the young one, and both me and my children looked up to an older woman as Auntie Edie. Now I'm the older one and the young women with small children make me the Auntie Nan.

☐   Society puts too much pressure on young women. In order to buy a house women are expected both to work and raise a family. The state should give better social back-up or be prepared to provide cheaper housing.

9

Most council house dwellers are young families with children, so obviously there will be a lot of problems related to children. The council should design with children in mind; it would cut down on vandalism and stop children wandering aimlessly. Without a woman at home there is need for back-up facilities, community centres and youth clubs that operate while parents work.

## Knickers and pots in the same sink

☐   The Briggate house looked out onto the River Calder and, although pleasant enough, was nothing like as good as the council house we moved into on Smith House Avenue in 1939. In the centre of Brighouse there was a physical closeness, five houses in a small court, and a neighbourliness. On the new council estate there was neighbourliness, but also friendliness and space; I could skip. Although I didn't have my own bedroom but had to share with one of the boys, we were no longer cramped.

☐   I lived in a back-to-back and moved into a council house on Whitwell Avenue in the 1930s. We had three girls and the house had three bedrooms. There was a bathroom and toilet, but no wash basin. For hot water, we had a back boiler — quite a luxury — but electricity costs were minimal, Elland Council had its own electricity in those days. Folk in other houses paid a shilling a week minimum and so much for each extra light.

After that, we moved into some red brick bungalows. The council had them purpose-built to get older families, whose children had left home, out of three-bedroomed houses. They wanted these for young families. The twenty red brick bungalows they built at that time are now part of a sheltered housing complex. We've grown old with them. The idea to build bungalows around a community hall is marvellous, but you can't get all the old

people to come in. The houses are good, but ready for modernising now. The baths are very rough-sided. They could do with handles on and we could do with low flush toilets instead of the old string pull.

There will always be a need for council housing, especially with the mortgages how they are now. They shouldn't build any more flats though — you can get lonely in them.

☐   I was born in a council house in 1940, one of the first in our area with a bath and running water. It had four bedrooms — we were a very big family, sixteen children. Mum and Dad and the babies slept in the one bedroom that had a fireplace. There were seven boys in the big bedroom. All the girls over puberty age slept in another and the little girls slept in the last one. When the older ones got married they brought their wives and husbands back. The only way then to get a house of your own was to move back with your parents into one that was already overcrowded and force the council to rehouse you.

Imagine having just one sink for all that lot, knickers and pots in the same sink.

☐   I was born in Smithy Street and lived in Sky Alley in a "kip house". My parents rented a furnished room there. They shared the kitchen and bathroom with six more people.

☐   When you've lived 74 years you have seen a lot. Our first house after we got married was a council house in Harley Place. I worked at Bottomleys' Sawmill then. We bought our bedroom suite with a tallboy and our dining room table and chairs at the Co-op in Brighouse in 1939. We've still got that furniture today.

We bought our house in 1947 for £100 and then we bought a house in Bridgend in 1958 for £450. We got a grant to put a bathroom into that one.

They pulled a lot of the houses down round us when they built the Green End Council Estate. It is a lovely estate. The

*Salterhebble Hill from Exley Bank c. 1920*

lawns are so well looked after, I reckon that alone has improved the value of my property.

## The Siddallers are coming

☐ At the end of Thomas Street there was a sheer wall which we used for various games. We would throw balls up, catch them behind our heads, bounce them under one leg; we had a routine of about eight different actions. We thoroughly enjoyed ourselves. You never see children doing that these days. I think for years there were the marks on the paving stones where we used to play games. We nearly wore them out with hopscotch.

☐ I lived in a little stone terraced house, number 21, half way up Page Hill. Facing the road, it had three windows and a brown front door with a step worn down by years of footsteps and scrubbing and donkey-stoning. Dickie Brier couldn't leave the milk on the door step, it was so concave. Instead, he'd put the blue earthenware jug, with a plate on top to keep the cats and the flies out, on the stone flag nearest the door, and God help you if you kicked it over.

Page Hill is no more than two hundred yards from top to bottom but it boasted three bonfires every fifth of November, defended to the death by two gangs and one private family. This family was posh, too, because their house was a farm on its own land and they had livestock — pigs, a cow, and hens.

We often went down to the beck which ran into Dapper Dam. It would be deep blue, and sometimes rusty red, depending on what dyeing had been going on. Sticklebacks lived in it but were not for catching at "plotting" time when we were busy planning and preparing for the best bonfire.

11

One Bonfire Night we were throwing bangers and chasing each other with fireworks. Richard McDermott, who didn't care for anything or anybody, had not seen me empty the powder out of one of the bangers, and put his hand down as I dropped a match on the powder. It went up like a flash and his hand was badly burned. They took him in the ambulance. I've told my own kids about it a hundred times.

☐    When I was a child we lived in Coronation Road and we'd never have anything to do with people from Siddall because they pinched our "plot". Before Bonfire Night we would go around collecting "plot", which was stuff to burn on the bonfire. The Siddallers would come up to Coronation Road to steal the stuff we'd collected and the cry would go up, "The Siddallers are coming!"

☐    Historically Halifax town spreads westwards from the Hebble Brook. There can be little westward development because the lie of the land is against it, it is too steep. The main roads go out from the area around the Parish Church like five fingers. Consequently there are a lot of old buildings in the centre and ribbon development along the major route ways. The big council house estates are on the outskirts; places like Abbey Park, Ovenden, Mixenden and Illingworth.

As time has passed the council house estates have grown and small settlements have virtually disappeared. At Luddendenfoot, for instance, there were sixty shops once, now there are about five.

☐    When I was a girl in the centre of Halifax, you could play in the street till nine o'clock and see no traffic come past. In Queen's Road we would be sledging in winter and you could come down Hanson Lane with no fear of traffic. Each little gang had its own gas lamps to play round. We would chalk all our names on these. We would then play a game called "touching

*Above Halifax Parish Church 1989*

*Gill Cliff*

12

*Old Market Street, Market Arcade*

iron". Someone was the catcher, and you'd run and touch a piece of iron, then another — grates and hydrants, the lot — but if you got caught before touching some iron, you were "on". There were other games. I used to sit on the fountain steps at the tram terminus, and count the cars with lady drivers. If we got up to ten we were doing well.

☐ It was possible to kick gas lamps on and off because the mechanism which lit the mantle was fragile. As kids, we sometimes caused the lights to be on all day and off all night. When I see lights left on on motorways I think there is nothing new in this world.

☐ Then of course there was electricity. Every child in a house with gas heard of the people who were gassed in their sleep, so electricity seemed a desirable luxury. Our bath and the toilet were together. When I was little, I continued to bathe in

front of the fire — running for cover behind some curtains if someone came unexpectedly. The privacy of a bathroom was something I really enjoyed as I got older. I didn't always get it. Once, when staying at a friend's who didn't have frosted glass, I was scared stiff when a face appeared at the window. Mind, I knew who it was.

## Most of the people you saw you knew

☐ They were happy days then. Everybody was willing to help one another and they were more neighbourly than people are now. We didn't have television, only wireless, and all the neighbours helped each other out.

When we were children we used to run errands for a penny, then we spent it on sweets or fish and chips. We would eat chips with fish bits under the gas lamps at

13

night. At Christmas we went round to my cousin's and other people's houses for parties, where we used to play games like charades, and sing and play the piano.

☐ When we first got married, we lived with my husband's parents until we got a house of our own. I didn't get on with them very well, so I was glad to move into my own house — but that was only two doors up on the same row.

☐ A lot go on about this neighbourliness and how good it was, as if people were naturally kinder. That wasn't my experience. I can remember rows, and drunks in the entry. People were so-called neighbourly because it was convenient. You were physically too close to be anything else.

☐ We moved from army accommodation into our own home in Sowerby Bridge. At first the neighbourhood was hard to settle in. It's very clannish and you have to fit in.

☐ During the war there were soldiers on lookout up Wainhouse Tower. My father was ill then and he used to take a walk there to sit on the seat and talk to them. They got very friendly with him and used to leave their kit with him when they went on leave. When my father died the soldiers lined the kerbside and saluted as his coffin passed by.

☐ Most of the people you saw, you knew. Foreigners you never saw. When Belgians got billeted up Stoney Lane we were told, "Think on, you don't go up there again." Once I went to London with my dad to the Speedway Final but usually you kept close to home. Of course I met foreigners when the evacuees from the Channel Islands came to stay.

☐ We were poorer but life was much simpler when I was young. I know, for a birthday, I'd be about seven or eight, I got a little, tiny gramophone. It was a little square one which someone had bought me, and some little records. It played all

*Fenton Road from Wainhouse Tower 1985*

the old songs and I had it for years. When I was a girl all the children round about used to come. I would take it outside and we'd have the gramophone run. I thought that was wonderful. We played it until it wore itself out.

I had a tea service, the cups were decent sized ones in pale blue. Everybody used to come to our house and I would make tea for them. Occasionally we would have a biscuit that we broke up into little bits, but that wasn't very often. We used to get cocoa and sugar, mix it up and then eat it on a spoon. At my age, I still like cocoa and sugar. It tastes very nice, the next thing to chocolate, you see.

## Walkie-talkie neighbourliness

☐ Me and my next door neighbour have taken neighbourliness into the modern age. So we could support each other after her husband died, we agreed that she would rap on the skirting if she felt low but after a time we decided that we could do better and fixed up a walkie-talkie system from one house to the other. At first it seemed a bit odd and we got confused, talking across each other. In the end I remembered the films and started to say "Over" or "Over and out."

☐ I applied to move to sheltered housing because they have a warden. I kept falling down. I used to have to knock on the skirting board at Talbot, now all I have to do is pull a string and the warden comes.

☐ In the 1930s we children would sit on the ledges of our houses with an intercom, actually two tin cans at either end of a piece of stick.

☐ I was brought up on a big council estate before and during the war. It wasn't rough though, not like the estates nowadays, I think it was the fifties when that trend started.

The only crime I can remember was two lads who stole bikes and were doing them up in a shed at the back of their house. The police came down and it was the talk of the neighbourhood for ages. It wouldn't cause much of a stir today. People were a lot closer then. My mother burned her hand badly and had to go into hospital for a few days, so the woman next door gave us our breakfast and a meal in the evening when we got home from school. You didn't think about it, it was just expected. That woman had eight kids of her own to look after.

In those days the older kids were expected to look after the younger ones; not just your own brothers and sisters but the rest of the little ones in the street. If we ever went off for a few hours or a day out, the older ones were responsible for getting the others back safe. There would be all hell to play if they didn't come back together.

☐ You made your own entertainment. When I was in my teens I was a cyclist, and then I started camping. I cycled with Halifax Clarion Cycling Club. We used to go camping, we once camped at Hardcastle Craggs on Christmas Day. It was a healthy life. There was nothing — there's still nothing — at Hardcastle Craggs but we used to make our own pleasure. You could roam in the wood and sit around a fire at night, talking and singing. Hardcastle Craggs was so far out that you couldn't get transport, you had to walk from the end of Midgehole. The best way of going was to go up Heptonstall Bank — Bunk it's called around here.

The only other entertainment was rollerskating at Gibson's Mill, and dancing down at Hebden Bridge for some of the older ones. I finished up as a motor cyclist, and I was secretary for Halifax Motor Cycling Club. One year we had a man from the Club represent Halifax in the T.T. Races in the Isle of Man.

☐ I played football and cricket, and as a

*Market Street, Hebden Bridge c. 1920*

*King Cross Lane 1912*

*Pace Egg Play, Sowerby 1900*

boy I carried bags for the William IV Pub League players. They played on Savile Park. I used to get a glass of lemonade in return.

King Cross Wesleyans used to have the best scout troop in Halifax – I'm bragging now – the 32nd troop. On Easter Monday we used to set off, and the first place we sang at was The Old King yard; that is pulled down now. Then we went up Warley Road, where it's built on now. We had our Whitsuntide treat, a bun, on Sandhall. They also had these big urns with coffee. When the Corporation started to build there we went to Fisher-Smith's up at Birdcage – they lent us their field for our Whitsuntide Treat. We still used to start at The Old King, come on down to Trafalgar, over Spring Edge, stop at Spring Edge and then make our way down the far side of the moor, down to Sir George Fisher-Smith's.

☐　We moved out of Lord Street into a council property when I was quite young. Mother reckoned to have the first washing machine in Elland – a Goblin – and therefore this was more appropriate property to show it off. Dad loved it. There was a garden front and back but because he couldn't keep hens the allotment was kept on. The only worm in the bud was the local sewage grate which surfaced in the front garden and spoiled his plan for roses. Nevertheless he still won the first or second prize for the best kept garden in the area.

☐　I used to go round the neighbours after school and get lists of shopping they wanted. Some gave me money to pay for shopping, others had it on weekly terms. I had a cart made from orange boxes with pram wheels on. I used to drag it on Queen's Road. On Friday night I collected 3d from each house. I was saving up for a bicycle. I saved up 27/6d for the one I wanted and Mum put the other 2/6d to it.

☐ We all knew one another. I mean, round here, what we used to call Back Lane, well, there used to be dozens of boys, more boys than girls really, and we all footballed together and "plotted" together and fought together. The 1939 War kicked that job... I lost a lot of friends.

☐ There were customs which made you know it was a neighbourhood. The young men had gone off fighting Mr Hitler, then one day a telegram boy came down the street. It was one of the Eastwood boys. The curtains closed. Then, all down the street, house after house closed its curtains as a sign of respect.

☐ We hadn't got much but what we had we shared. There wasn't a child in our street who did not know where the buns and biscuits were. The little lad next door would come in when he could barely walk, let alone talk, and point, "Owen! Owen! Biscuits."

## A frog called Pestilence

☐ Even in the forties council estates could contain a range of characters. On one side of us there was a homosexual man, on the other side a transvestite, and across the road was a girl who showed everyone a wedding ring and said she was engaged to her father.

Once we received a note made up of letters cut from magazines saying, "Watch your windows, the man next door is queer." He never bothered us, why should he, he was alright. It was the same with the man who dressed up in women's clothing; actually he was very intelligent. His wife told my mam that he had expensive lingerie and underskirts. He also had five children. I once saw him out all dressed up, he was exceptionally tall, and he frightened me. Now we have got more tolerant, and that's a good thing. He never hurt anyone and always used men's toilets.

The man across the road was a different matter. His wife was ill but that was no excuse, whatever a judge might say, for having sex with his teenage daughter.

☐ I am 96. I lived in Victoria Avenue for 57 years. We had a lovely garden overlooking the cemetery and there was no trouble from children or old folk but plenty of fun on those long summer nights long ago. One man I remember used to say, "Old Anderson is trying to get up to tell you lot to hop it" – that when old Mr Anderson had been buried forty years.

☐ I had called at the flat several times, to dress an injured toe on my district nursing round. Jed answered my knock. I suspected he was wearing little more than a black satin kimono. His hair, however, was his most arresting feature, shocking pink and arranged in a stiff halo around his face. He was a good-looking young man with a baby's bottom complexion enhanced by powder and rouge. His long-lashed blue eyes were skilfully mascaraed. He wore a diamond stud in both nose and ear.

Despite the make-up and the hairdo I gathered that he had been in bed and his dreamy spaced-out demeanour suggested he might have been smoking dickipoggy cigarettes. The fact that the flat was filled with a redolent smog helped to confirm this notion.

Inside the flat which was painted in black and white, the curtains were never open. Jed kept some rather interesting pets. There was a great big hairy spider called Plague and a fat psychedelic-coloured frog called Pestilence. He fed Pestilence locusts kept in a rather unreliable box on top of its vivarium. He had a massive hi-fi system and various queer things, like animal bones and satanic memorabilia, lying around. Myself, I was more frightened of the locusts and the spider than I was of Jed.

☐ I'm proud to be a Yorkshire person, I

*Backs, Elland 1989*

*Whitwalk, Todmorden 1900*

like the idea. Perhaps it is because it is unfashionable down south to be a northerner. We are down to earth and normal, you see, so when I move off to university I have chosen to go to one in Yorkshire, Sheffield University. It's like Halifax, stone built with plenty of trees not far from beautiful countryside, and like Halifax, it's the open people who make it.

☐ You hear a lot of stories about how the early council tenants treated their houses. Most are a bit fanciful but as an insurance man you see a lot. Coal in the bath, I have seen that. One of my colleagues reckons to have gone into a kitchen and when she asked why the pony was sleeping on the hearth rug the man replied that it was a three-bedroomed house but as yet he hadn't worked out a way to get it upstairs.

☐ This man had trouble with his television. He was a big brussen man so when he phoned the rental service he threatened them. You know the sort of thing, "You'll come now or you'll know about it." Well, of course they didn't, people don't respond to threats, but by Tuesday, five days later, they thought they would go round and take a look.

The man was a bit subdued by this time but when they tried the set he was right, it didn't work. They therefore took a look at the fuse in the plug. It was okay. Then they decided to trace the wire back.

Behind the settee there was a dead alsatian. He had chewed through the electric cable. Dead all weekend, and his owner had not noticed.

☐ I was born in the country and I wanted nothing more than to live on an estate. It was the neighbourliness that was important to me, you felt so isolated in the country. On an estate "mischief night" and "plot night" meant something.

It was only when I got to Whinney Hill that I realised I was mistaken. The houses are too spread out and there is little sense

*Large rabbits, two shillings c. 1920*

of community. Then there's the top end and the bottom end. There's a big divide.

☐ The trouble with council housing is the neighbours are coming and going all the time. You just get to know somebody and they move.

I very rarely see my neighbours. The only time I see them is through the window and the only time we talk is when we pass but they're nice folk. If it hadn't been for the wife's ill health we wouldn't have come here. Mind you, they condemned the old estate and knocked it down.

☐ We lived with my parents after we were married. You didn't have long to wait for a house then. We brought up our children here, in our council house, there were seven of them.

I suppose we could have bought it a few years ago, but we've always been happy. They are modernising these houses soon and they're putting gas central heating in. It should be nice. Three of my children are buying their own homes. It takes two wage packets to buy a house.

When we first moved in there were lots of kids around here, but as the years have gone by, the estate has got quieter. It's happening again though. Two elderly women have moved out by me and have been replaced by young families. Life goes on.

☐ We've been living in a council house in Illingworth for the last twelve years. The children are grown up now and most of the people on the estate are in our age group. Buying a house gives you opportunities if you are young enough. We are being well looked after as tenants, the council come out very quickly to do repairs.

## Some things in those dustbins

☐ I only stuck the caretaker's job for four months, but it was an education. I suppose that I was surprised to get it, being only nineteen, unemployed and a woman but I think I did well at the interview. "How would you cope with a difficult tenant? Would you keep coming back to us?" they asked. "No," I said, "I would try to sort it out myself. I would say to people, 'I've got a job to do and if you don't keep the place tidy you'll get me into trouble.' That will be sufficient." It was sufficient with a lot, but not all, of course, because out of every six there was one who was pretty hopeless.

My job was to keep things tidy. You'd have to see that the bins were kept tidy, sweep leaves, clear snow and look out that the surrounding areas were well kept. Some would throw everything out of the window. It would be tea bags first but then it would build up to full dinners. Not many, of course, but enough.

You learned how to treat them. They would talk to each other so you didn't make a direct approach. You would say, "It's terrible but I'll have to do something. I could report her or then again I suggest that she has a dustbin in her kitchen." I knew that sort of thing would get back. Next time I went − she was a good lass really but she didn't have standards − all the tea bags had been collected from underneath the kitchen window and the mould on the window ledge had been wiped away. I think that it is better doing it that way and not risk a smack in the mouth.

☐ We British seem to have no sense of obligation to our environment, there's litter everywhere, dogs are running wild, fouling the pavement. Take the Piece Hall, it could be such an attractive tourist place but there is rubbish everywhere. We must be champions in ignoring litter bins.

☐ In some parts you almost say that everybody messes and no-one cares but then every estate has that. People know the bad streets. In the old days it was

*New fences, Gerrard Street*

council policy to dump awkward families and single parents together into sin cities. Later, they would put a difficult household in the centre of a crescent in the hope that the district would lift to better standards. It never did.

That's partly because people make excuses. It's *their* job to mend things, never the tenants'. This leads to stupid situations, and the council's attitude doesn't help. One of my neighbours went to a lot of trouble to maintain his fence. He made a reasonable job of it, so when the council came to put up fences for homes where people didn't bother, they left his alone. He was the only one to keep his old fence, and yet he was the only person on the road paying full rent.

☐ Our estate in Siddall used to be lovely, I lived there for thirty-odd years. It's a mix of council and private. Unfortunately now they put in every Tom, Dick, Harry. We get lots of families with kids, they are trying to mix them in but all it does is drag down the neighbourhood.

It's especially tough on the old folk in the bungalows since they removed their garden gates and opened it all up. The old people don't feel safe and there's no longer a warden to look after them either. This estate was desirable once, you used to have points to get on, now you need points to get off!

☐ Council house tenants are just like tenants in private housing, so of course they want to better themselves. The difference is, you are entirely at the mercy of the council's timetable so you hold back on the decorating and the new carpet, and wait. Sometimes the wait is a long one; you are in a state of limbo. Sometimes the dream home you always wanted never comes. Waiting is part and parcel of being a council tenant. You get used to it, I suppose.

☐ I could open Wainhouse Tower — this was before the war — using a piece of wire. We'd be after pigeons' eggs. We went on to the balcony at the bottom edge of the crown and by the time we got to the first landing, shouting and bawling as we went, the bobby had seen us and by the time we got to the bottom he'd be waiting for us. Mind, he never locked us up.

In those days, if anyone caught you doing wrong, they would give you a clip round the ear. You can't give kids a clip round the ear these days, or you are up for assault. If you broke a window then you didn't run off, you went and told the householder. Then you got another belt off your mother when you told her.

☐ I like it round here really, though there's not much to do at night. Me and me mates go drinking in Halifax sometimes. I'd like to get this job crushing plastics in Westvale, it would be more interesting than working in a record or clothes shop.

I wouldn't mind living in a council house. I'd see it as a step to owning my own. I'd like a sixteen-bedroomed mansion, and to be a millionaire by tomorrow.

☐ I've seen some things in those dustbins, I can tell you; dead rats, maggots, but the worst thing you will find in dustbins are unwrapped disposable nappies. I spent a week before my holidays doing everything possible; bleach, disinfectant, the lot. I wasn't away more than three days. When I got back the rubbish was up to the top of the wall and the black rubbish bags were still folded up in the bottom of the bins. There were wasps everywhere. I started to clean up but I was physically sick. In the end they got the chief man from the Calderdale dustbin men out. He was disgusted.

After I had left they started evicting people, and things got better. By that time though I had had enough. I decided that although the money was quite good I couldn't take going round and cleaning up after people.

☐ As soon as the refuse bags are folded over the handles you see doors open and people scuttle out and collect them for their individual swing bins.

## Computers don't visit everybody

☐ It was lovely being a rent collector in the old Elland UDC days twenty five years ago. Most people paid their rents without any fuss at all. Melrose Court was remarkable, everybody was always paid up. It was a joy. Every book balanced right across the columns.

In the last days of a year people would be queuing at the Council offices to pay. They liked to enter the New Year with a clean rent card.

On every estate there was someone who had a cup of tea ready for the rent collector but then most local government functions were more human. Our boss used to say, "As rent collectors you are the first council officers people come into contact with and therefore you are the first ambassadors." Because of that you had more time for people. One man has delivered a batch of mince pies to me for the last twenty years.

☐ As a rent collector I have measured lino, made toast and tea for hundreds, and dressed endless numbers of old ladies. In many ways we were social workers because every week we visited every house. Now it is more specialised. Computers are remarkable but they do not visit everybody.

☐ In the old days the council took very little interest in people's taste. No money was given to help redecorate. People got council colours. Once a complete batch of houses were done out in battleship grey because we acquired a consignment.

☐ They are modernising our council

house. It's fifty years old, so it needs a bit doing to it. I wish they'd consulted me though. They are putting in a bathroom upstairs but I need mine downstairs, my husband is 72 and crippled, he can't go upstairs.

☐ The council did the ceilings with that grey plaster, which means that when you emulsion the ceilings you have to go over them again and again.

I papered downstairs with pink, grey, white — my mates said it looked like a mortuary, but I like different shades of grey. I did the little lad's bedroom with Thomas The Tank Engine, it cost £4.95 a roll although the council only gave us £12 per room towards the cost of redecorating. They have a rule as well that you can't put woodchip paper or anaglypta in every room, or just emulsion every room, and they come to check it.

☐ Every year the authority gets more remote. In the office we are encouraged to *Think Calderdale* but actually people round here don't even think Elland; they think as Stainlanders or Hollywell Greeners.

☐ I worked for Brighouse Council in the early 1960s as a rent collector. In 1960 it was nineteen shilling and a penny for a two-bedroomed house and a pound a week for a three-bedroomed one. My round was three hundred houses. Out of this number, I'd say thirty to forty left the rent in the book on the table with the back door open for me to collect.

☐ My gran's rent book was always up to date but when they went decimal the rent collector reckoned that she was a halfpenny in arrears. This really upset her. Grandad went wild. She was all for settling but he was not having that. Instead he set up a stool by the dustbin and thereafter left the book plus the money there for the rent man to collect.

☐ I live on the Smith House Estate. The

*Elland council offices*

size of my house is okay but the damp is terrible. The walls are green with mould but the council is trying to tell me it is condensation. Now they keep promising me new central heating. The estate is alright, though everyone keeps themselves to themselves. It's handy for schools. There's Cliffe Hill Infants School and Hipperholme and Lightcliffe Secondary School. I used to live on Whinney Hill in a nice flat. We moved when I had my daughter, for I already had our Raymond and it was a one-bedroomed flat. I'd move back to Whinney Hill if I could.

My dad lives in a house here as well. He went out one day and when he came back the council had painted his house green. They never even consulted him. He was really mad, he doesn't even like green. They either painted them green or cream, they're horrible colours.

The council are alright with minor things. I had a leaking tap and they came out right away. You wouldn't get that with a private landlord. But it's the big things you can't get done. As a single-parent family we're reliant on the council.

☐ The council will get repairs done but they don't have their own maintenance staff any more. It's cowboys now, private contractors who are not bothered about doing the job properly, they just move on elsewhere.

☐ My first memory of council housing is as a very young girl sitting on a box in an almost empty room toasting beans over a single ring and eating baked beans. Dad had thrown Mother and us four girls out and we were being housed by the council.

It was the most depressing scene I have ever set eyes on. This small room, with dog muck in the hallway outside, was a council flat.

In those days you could get married at sixteen, and be on the pill, but as a woman you could not have your own council property without someone acting as guarantor.

☐ I bought a portable gas fire to help heat my two-bedroomed flat on Field Lane. It only had one gas fire in it and I used to go to my parents' house to get warm in the winter. The council got half way up the road putting central heating in and they ran out of money.

☐ My daughter moved into a flat in Sunny Bank Terrace. The rent is £30 per week but because she is on a low income she pays £27 per week. She needs a car to get to work so she hasn't much money to play with. Most of the other tenants are elderly, it is a quiet place and she likes it there. My other two daughters have bought their own houses, one down Huddersfield Road and one by Barkisland Hall. Lord Kagan used to live there. It was his factory that made Gannex macs. My friend worked there and used to make the special orders in the factory. She made coats and luggage for the Queen and the Duke of Edinburgh.

☐ I think a lot of people abuse council property. People who have a lot of money could afford to buy their own houses leaving the council houses for the more needy.

I'm a Royal Mental Nurse. Patients are leaving our charge in hospital and they are going out to live in flats and bedsits owned by private landlords. They should be going into council-run properties, not to private landlords who are only interested in the one thing. I would like sheltered houses with different underprivileged groups integrated with older people, and people with special needs. This would give people who we discharge a better chance, we cannot really monitor them adequately. They might be in a bedsit flat and only be visited once a week by a community nurse and a social worker. This is not enough. I would say that fifteen percent of our patients are motivated to go into the world outside, the other eighty five percent are institutionalised. I work with people who still talk in shillings.

*Sowerby Bridge 1989*

They are not prepared to be discharged into the community at large. There should be more hostels for the mentally ill and there should be council property there for the underprivileged. At least with the council there are safeguards.

☐ We're a one parent family living in a two-bedroomed flat in Highfield Road. I worked in Woolies' in Commercial Road for two years. When I worked full time I had to pay £26 a week rent for my flat, but most of the time I worked part time. It came to the point where if I worked a certain amount of hours in the week I'd have to pay £2.94 a week and if I worked an hour more I'd have to pay £26 per week. This went on for two years and it got in a right state. They didn't even know how much I owed them. I couldn't cope and if my parents hadn't paid £200 off in arrears I could have been out on the street. It is very unfair.

## With folk who I like and a goat in the garden

☐ I have lived in a council house with my family all my life. When it came on the market my parents bought it because they liked it, and they thought it was a nice house to buy.

I couldn't afford to buy my own house so I would hope to get a council house when I leave home, but I wouldn't want a high-rise flat. On the whole I think I'd rather buy a house.

☐ I'm 18, I've just done A-levels. I'd like to own my own house but I don't know when that will be. I'd like a cottage in the country. I live in a farmhouse with my mum and dad. There's lots of room but we don't get on. My friend is sharing a rented house – maybe I'll be able to move there in a year or so.

☐ What I want to know is, what will happen to people like me when everything goes private? There were three girls in our family sharing one bedroom, single beds pushed against the wall. I was the eldest at nineteen and my sister was only five. There was no privacy.

The council agreed that this wasn't right and quickly got me a single person's flat. It was not on grounds of health but on social grounds that I got the necessary points. I cannot believe that a private landlord will act with that sort of consideration. They will reckon it's my parents' fault for having three girls.

☐ The Government are saying that young people should live with their parents until they get married. If young people fall out with their parents they are in trouble; where are they going to live? There are no private flats round here that they could afford to rent and there is only one hostel-type accommodation, The Crow's Nest, where people are only expected to stay six weeks at a time and then they are supposed to move on. I've worked with young girls who have become pregnant so that they can get a flat from the council.

☐ I'm living at home at the moment. It's a nice house, on a street on the side of a hill, no-one looking in on you. I lived in a rented house when I was at college – that was alright. I didn't go anywhere near halls of residence. I wouldn't pay £15 for a room that size. I wanted to be in a house. If I got my own place I'd want to live in the outskirts of a town and commute. It all depends on where I work. I've got some interviews down south. I want to live in a big house but if I go down south it'll have to be a small one. I'll probably knock all the walls down and have one big room.

☐ I used to live in a commune with eighteen other people. The idea was great and we had a rota, so that all tasks were shared. It's difficult for so many people to be committed though. If just one falls down on the system, it all begins to break up.

*The baseball team and friends 1989*

It's even more difficult to become self-sufficient, but the ideas, economics, resources and company all appeal to me. The idea of shutting the front gate and being with folk who I like, and a goat in the garden, really appeals to me.

☐ I live in Illingworth with my mother, brother and two sisters in two houses that were knocked into one by the council. They are for big families. There were ten of us when we first came. We've got six bedrooms, two bathrooms and two toilets. The house is damp and in bad need of modernising. It is very difficult to keep up with, now most of the others have left. The family suffers from asthma and it's not healthy for us. We've got a gas fire downstairs but cold bedrooms. All council houses should have central heating. There should be more consideration for people with ill health, especially children.

I came to the community centre because I'm on an ET training scheme. I serve lunches to the old folk and help look after them while they're here. I've tried to get a proper job, but I suffer from asthma like the rest of my family and find it difficult to get the jobs I want.

☐ When I first left home I lived in a one-bedroomed flat. What made me feel really independent was having my own loo to flush.

## Don't let the walls come in on you

☐ I know they think we are nuisances but pensioners have the right to the same facilities as everyone else. I live on Lower Edge, Elland, in a flat. We've got a warden and we're on an intercom system. The warden is really nice and she calls in mornings and tea times. Some of the others put on her a bit. She has to shut her intercom off when she's not on duty.

Three people were burgled round here

28

recently. They think pensioners have got money but it's only the money to pay the next bills. They say we haven't got enough crime and vandalism to have a bobby on the beat here. They suggested us getting a neighbourhood watch scheme but that's foolishness, we're too old.

It's lonely being a widow, there's times when I'd be glad of someone to have a good row with. There are times I've felt the walls coming in on me. I got a little Cairn Terrier called Penny. She must be nine now but she still acts like a pup. I have to do these exercises to keep me moving like sitting up and shaking my arms. Penny will sit in the other chair and shake her paws at me. She's marvellous. I don't know what I'll do if she goes before me.

☐   We live in Chapel Croft. They are council flats that have been open about ten years. The flats are alright but you have to come into town to the shops. There's only a post office round here. I think the flats are too dear. We pay £32 a week and my pension is only £42 while my wife gets £23. That's a big hole in your money. I hand my pension over in the rent office.

☐   I come to the community centre to get out of the house. I get fed up on my own, too many memories. I live in a council flat on the ground floor. We got it when my wife was living because she couldn't walk. I think I'd take my chances on the first floor if I could swap.

I lived down Siddall when I was single. When I got married our landlady asked us to leave due to overcrowding. The wife already had four kids. We got our first council house in Wheatley. As we got older we decided to move down Ovenden to be near the family. The only trouble is they don't come round much. I've got to go and see them.

☐   When I left school I went into the building trade as an apprentice plasterer. When I spoke to my mother she was

*Elland council flats. 1989*

*New Street, Elland c. 1900*

apprehensive as you might expect. "It's a rough trade,"she said, "be civil but don't take their habits, swearing, gambling things like that." The first day we went down to the pub and one of the men bet another that he could eat a dozen pies; he didn't, he ate thirteen.

Well, time passed and I became a master builder. I had raised a lot of money for the Maurice Jagger Centre for the Disabled and Elderly. One day I was busy in the shell of the building when I saw two people knocking on the window. I let them in and they looked around although I didn't know them from Adam. They watched me for a bit.

"By gum, you're good at that. Do you fancy doing some building for us? We'll pay well."

"I don't know about that," I said, "I think that the wife might object."

They watched for a bit longer and then the woman said, "I don't know about yon chap's name on the front. It's your name that ought to be up there."

"It is mine," I said.

☐   I have been a council tenant for forty two years. I live above the Community Hall now. The flat is not very well designed and too small. The front room is L-shaped and if you sit in a certain place you can't see the television.

Sheltered housing is smashing. They should build more, especially in this area. Calderdale has the second highest ratio of old people in local authorities in Britain.

There isn't much trouble with kids. If you talk to them nice enough they're off. There's no more abuse from kids on council estates than on private ones.

☐   The council ought to think about how to control kids. Kids don't have a bedtime now. They jump over the walls, spoil the gardens and flowers and stare in the windows. It's important to have better gates and walls. We'd even pay for them.

☐ I'm a Geordie. I've been here thirty five years. I moved here to be near the wife's parents. I'm a boiler firer by trade. I owned my own house and I was on the Elland Neighbourhood Council. It's a voluntary organisation that meets once a month and deals with people's complaints about the council. We would air people's complaints, it didn't matter if they were council tenants or private owners. I used to have a good contact in the *Courier* highlighting our complaints. I could cause a stir when I got a bee in my bonnet.

☐ Neighbourliness on the social level tends to decline as you go up the social scale. Sadly, it appears that much of the buying and selling of houses is geared towards social climbing. "Environmental neighbourliness", for want of a better term, then takes over — the care of parks, open spaces and grass verges. Then of course "neighbourhood watch schemes" are set up. It's the sense of community of the well-to-do: Put up signs and hope that the burglars are of the softer run and go to steal off someone else.

Gill Cliff

*Gibbet Lane 1989*

*I have a Vision of The Future, chum,*
*The workers' flats in fields of soya beans*
*Tower up like silver pencils, score on score.*

John Betjeman

# HEROES FITTED INTO HOMES?

*Planning And Government Policy*

## MBE — Making a Bugger of Elland

☐ In the 1960s they got the idea — from Corbusier was it? — that people lived better when they were close together. In Sheffield they had built enormous complexes at Kelvin so they decided that they would do the same in the centre of Elland. They ripped out a lot of the derelict, picturesque buildings and put up the flats. They completely transformed the place.

The town clerk at the time got an MBE for it. People reckoned that it meant Making a Bugger of Elland.

☐ People will make derogatory remarks about the man responsible for the blocks of flats which dominate Elland's centre but actually his hands were tied. He realised that something had to be done and he was a man who could do things. A forthright man, he was caught by the planning regulations of the period.

He was able to get on with a wide variety of people and had a remarkable memory for names. He would go up to someone who he had met ten years earlier and address them by name. They wouldn't have a clue who he was. He would exercise this facility and amuse himself.

☐ The area they demolished to make the New Elland was a mixture of cottages and quality housing. Some of those houses were good, particularly those in Westgate; houses like that of Elland's historian, Lucy Hammerton. Others were poor and needed to come down.

I'm not the sort who argues that it was unnecessary to rebuild. No money was spent in the war years and much was beyond reasonable repair. Unfortunately the regulations in the late 1950s required you to sweep away the lot in order to get the grant. If you had to demolish a bungalow like Dr Greenwood's, built no earlier than the 1920s, I should think, and called *Bon Accord*, then you did so. Today your planning can be sensitive or site specific; that wasn't the case in 1960.

Thirty years ago planners thought in terms of the large scale visionary plan. No one seemed to recognise that by turning a street through 180 degrees and placing it on its end, so that it went into the sky, you were doing little to alter high density living. A man was brought in from Manchester and asked to present a scheme. He was a clever man, and if his plan had been followed through in its entirety, then it would have looked better but only half was built. The other half remains a car park to this day. Of course there were mistakes, especially in the choice of building materials, and we are paying that cost. The extent of weathering in this climate, for instance, was underestimated.

The sad thing for me is that we were too progressive. If New Elland had happened ten years later when planning regulations were more sensitive to particular needs, when preservation was given more status, then we would be living in something every bit as attractive as Heptonstall.

☐ When I came to Elland as a young headmaster in 1952, the area which was demolished to make way for the new development was still standing. Much of it was of historical interest. New Street, for instance, was one of the first to be built as a street and not just as a collection of houses. That was in 1790. It was mixed housing with great community spirit. New Street won the best decorated street in 1914 and also in 1918. Prosperous mill owners' houses were mixed in with

33

*Westgate, Elland c. 1900*

*Station Lane, Holywell Green c. 1900*

*Textile workers housing, Copley*

smaller dwellings. Of course the mill owners themselves had moved up-market into areas like Victoria Road somewhat earlier perhaps in the 1920s.

There wasn't much to do in a through-school in those days — a bit of needlework for the girls, a little woodwork for the boys — so I got down to local history. This meant I went to the old Parish records. We are fortunate that Elland has some of the oldest in the country and that they had been printed up. People go on about women working, they have always worked round here. Two women, for instance, are recorded in the fourteenth century poll tax returns as Websters, that is weavers. When we looked up the names in the church records, eight of the class of twenty four children had the same names as people on the front page of the four hundred year old register. Names like Gledhill, Hopkinson, Ramsden, Marsden, Helwell, Bottomley, Hoyle and Woodhead, all well-known Elland names,

were there. The streets that were knocked down in 1962 were inhabited by families who had lived on that patch of earth for centuries.

☐ What I like about people from Elland is they do not sit down and wait for life to catch up with them. Like many Calderdale people they have an independence of outlook. They are progressive. When they want a new road they commission a pioneer of road building, Blind Jack Metcalfe, to build one; when they want a canal they call in another famous Yorkshireman, John Smeaton.

Like everywhere else around here we suffered when textiles went into decline in the late 1960s but we weren't down for long. Workshops and mills opened to produce cricket bats, computers and, of all things, canoes. Who would have associated Elland with canoes?

What I think makes the people secure is that they are sure of their history.

☐ Calderdale was fortunate in having some very good housing for working people. Well before the council was able to build, well before Saltaire even, Colonel Akroyd had built well for his workers at Akroydon. Then there was Copley and later the planned industrial housing up King Cross.

These industrialists were socially conscious. I know, for instance, that the independent Copley Co-operative was paying a divi of half a crown in the pound when my mother was a girl.

☐ At Akroydon in the mid nineteenth century they built after thinking about people's needs. They had a school called The Shed School, a library and allotments. In the centre there was also open space with benches for an old men's parliament.

☐ There is nothing new about planning. The Crossleys built the Woothill Park area for their workers back in the mid nineteenth century with considerable attention to their needs. When you look at the blueprints you see that the houses are marked to show clear use. There is a boys' room, a girls' and a parents' room. Every house also has an ash closet in its own back yard and a cellar with a copper. There was even a W.C.

In those days many employers lived close to their employees. Cromwell and Milton Terraces are less than two hundred yards from the family's magnificent town house, Bellevue. Of course the contrast is spectacular and can be well recognised today because a big company, FKI, have just restored the house to its former state. It must have cost a million pounds. The wallpaper alone is £30 a length. Yet you can't help wondering if you would get a better cultural environment if people on a variety of incomes were closer together. Today it's easy to avoid going into slum areas, to avoid the ghettos. They also built People's Park at a time when few philanthropists were thinking about a wider concept of amenity.

It is reckoned that they built the almshouses side on to the front of the house so that they could block off the view of the town.

☐ I live in John Crossley Almshouses on King Cross Lane. They are about 150 years old now and were built by John Crossley who owned Dean Clough Mills. He was a big Methodist and at that time you had to be a big Methodist to get into the Almshouses. They were still funny about Catholics and Salvation Army then. People got ten shillings a week to live there, and a table, chair and bed. They had to get permission to go out at night.

The Almshouses are built in a square with gardens in the middle. There's a face like a gargoyle outside every door and we get a lot of students coming to paint them.

They are owned by the Trustees of the Crossley Estate now and we pay rent. They used to be like little houses with bedrooms, but they've been converted into flats. When I applied, I had to get a vicar's signature to say I was a Christian. Then I was accepted by the Trustees' Committee.

☐ There was a company in Ovenden called Wilson's Lathes. The owner's wife was Laura Wilson. She was a big Labour Party woman, a good woman, and she had some houses built for working class folk in Pye Nest, between Halifax and Sowerby Bridge. They were two-up two-down terraced houses, four in a block.

Ours was on Atalanta Terrace and we got it through the Labour Party. There was an advantage in knowing people. My wife was a trade union organiser and "keeping t'band in t'nick" as they say. I joined the Party as well.

We were the first occupiers in 1929, we paid £410 at two pound odd a month. Laura Wilson paid the deposit, then we paid her back. They were marvellous houses; inside toilet and bathroom with hot running water fired by a back boiler. There was electricity in every room, a coal fire in the front room and a gas fire in the kitchen.

## Aachen Way goes through houses

☐ The town planners have got a lot to answer for. They are to blame for causing a lack of good-neighbourliness by forcing people to live on top of one another. Everybody has the right to space, the freedom to move around easily, and above all privacy when they need it. A good neighbourhood is being able to walk down the street in the morning and say "hello" in the knowledge that you get on with your neighbours.

☐ The problem with council estates is that there is little variety when it comes to shops. When I was a boy, living in King Cross, you would never think of going into the centre of Halifax. There was Barker's chocolate shop, and where Aachen Way is there was a bank. My grandfather had a blacksmith's shop, this was about 1917/18 in Rushworth and Firth's yard. Then there was "German John's", he sold cooked meats. I think his real name was John Alfred Steinmetz.

☐ Down on the Moor on Thomas Street West there was the Big Six pub. There was going to be a brewery, and the Big Six was going to sell the beer, they were going to brew beer there. The front of the house they were going to use faces on to Savile Park just below Ingram Street. It's made into flats now. Then there was a Penny Bank, where you came from the corner of Burnley Road. In my early days a policeman used to stand where the fountain was. Jim Lawless, the greengrocer, and John Kennedy, the barber, saw more accidents happen at King Cross than the policeman on point duty. They were at the junction of Rochdale Road, Burnley Road and Warley Road.

I think we had the first barbecued chicken place in Halifax!

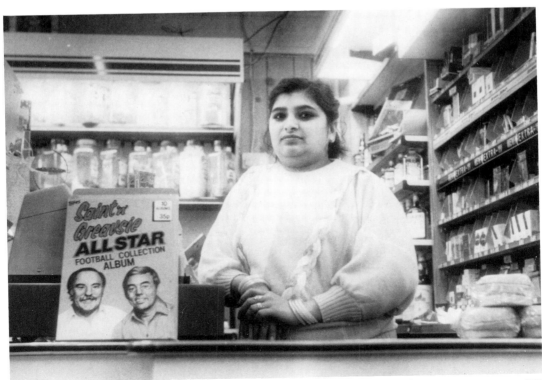

*The Spring Gardens Convenience Store 1989*

*Southgate, Elland*

☐ King Cross from the Co-op down to the garage hasn't altered so much. The shops maybe have altered. Now there are no traditional shops like there used to be except Swires the chemist's. His brother used to pull my teeth out, down Free School Lane. The area also used to have a lot of small engineering places. There was one that made ovens for bakehouses. Another one used to make model Ferraris out of plastic. That's a long time since, we could never afford them. Bancroft's used to make bunting and flags. There were all sorts of little businesses round here, like KX Ladies, Dan Gethin's Tripe Shop, and Driver's at the bottom of Wainhouse Road. McLachlan's the confectioners, Mrs Lister's the drapers and Madame Oldroyd's dancing school used to be down bottom of Walker Street in a house where the bank is now. There was a little square of houses called Warneford Square off Haugh Shaw Road. It was named after a man who shot a Zeppelin down in the

Great War. The butcher's shop there shut up at six o'clock, then opened again selling beer! All the houses down by the garage were pulled down for this road widening job. Aachen Way goes through the houses we once lived in.

☐ There were lots of little shops in the old areas that were really houses with the front room portioned off by a counter in front of a curtain. They sold sweets and chocolate. We used to go in and ask if they had any broken biscuits. If they replied, "Yes, love," we would shout, "Well, mend them!" as we ran off.

☐ When we first got married we lived in an old cottage. It had a living room, one bedroom and a cellar with no drainage. We rented it from a Mr Farrar of Farrar's Mills. I never saw Mr Farrar though, it was somebody else who collected the rent, which was 8/- a week. We burned coal and I cooked on a fire oven. I had to do the laundry in a bowl in the living room and the washing was hung to dry there. It was nice and warm but when we got children it was no good to us. I wouldn't go back to that house. I'm in a one-bedroomed council flat now. I've lived there fourteen years and I was on the waiting list three years to get it.

☐   I moved up here from the south. I like it because of the way the streets are laid out. The houses don't all face the street and there's lots of unmade and unadopted roads, lots of cul de sacs. My ideal house would be one that's very thoroughly insulated to cut down the energy bills. Also I'd like it to be near to work so I don't have to use a car. As a member of the Green Party I'd most like to see more housing being built in infill areas in the towns not in villages. The present policy changes the character of the villages and the inner urban areas get more run-down.

## Sucking oranges in my ears

☐   Services are essential for a good neighbourhood. No matter how friendly the people are, you need the facilities to keep people happy. Shops, public transport and easy access all must play their part. It's no good having lovely neighbours if you can't get to the shops.

☐   It is not only the absence of shops on a modern estate, another weakness in the planning is that no one seems to have planned for entertainment. When I was young there were cinemas to help you get out of the rut. They reckon people are deserting the television now and going back to the pictures. You can't do that easily on a modern estate.

☐   Saturday night was the night for the cinema but you couldn't go straight in. You queued down the side of the cinema and along the front to the doorway. There'd be a commissionaire stood there — pompous, you know. "Two seats," he'd say and two people would go in, but even these didn't get into the cinema. They had to go into another waiting room till there were two seats in the actual cinema. You had to wait about an hour to see a film in the town cinemas.

In King Cross one lad would go in and

*Theatre Royal and Palace Theatre, Halifax c. 1905*

unlock the back door to let his friends in. In the Cosy Cinema in the 1920s there was a man who kept an eye on the kids and told them to be quiet. Kids were given an orange or bag of sweets for when they were in. It was 3d to go in. Charlie Chaplin was a favourite, and there was a little orchestra in the front playing music to the sob scenes. The Kingston Cinema was great for teenagers. In the balcony the seats were double, like little settees. There you could have a cuddle!

☐ I used to go dancing on Saturday nights at St Paul's Sunday School. Then there was the Palladium, which they put up to three halfpence, so we went on to the Cosy on Queen's Road where it was still only a penny. We kept our halfpence for sweets. We also went to the Kingston. The organist there was bald, and people used to throw chewing gum at his bald head. We used to see Pearl White. It doesn't seem five minutes when you look back.

☐ My dad liked the pictures. There was no television or anything then and I used to go to the pictures with Dad while Mum was at work. We went to the Palladium on Monday and the Kingston on Tuesday. You hadn't to talk to Dad at the pictures. There were matinees on Saturdays for children. Dad once took my uncle Freddy who said, "Never again. Kids were wiping their feet on me and sucking oranges in my ears."

☐ There was dancing at the Queen's Hall, but we used to go dancing twice a week at Madame Oldroyd's on King Cross where Dr Davidson's surgery used to be. There was a club for Sunday night dancing. You had to be a member, otherwise the police would intervene for dancing on a Sunday.

☐ When I was a lad living on the Ovenden Estate there was a lot more to do than there is now but this I do know, you can't plan for entertainment. Youth clubs have their place but you cannot solve boredom by throwing money at it.

When I was young in the early 1950s much that went off revolved round the chapels. You could only attend Brownies, Guides or Scouts if you attended a service on a Sunday. The football leagues for young people were all related to chapel attendance; no chapel, no football. You had the same obligation if you wanted to go camping at Appletreewick, Gargrave or Knaresborough. It was the same with the Bethel Boys' Brigade Pantomime. You could only be in it if you had been to Sunday Service.

This pantomime was started in 1937 and went on until 1984. The routine was always the same. It took place at the end of January and ran to eleven performances. I've known fourteen coaches come from as far away as Keighley — twelve miles away. By the 1980s a production would be costing about £800, and remember that by that time we had most of the things we needed, like costumes and lights. At that time we would come out of it with a profit of £1000. Upwards of two thousand people were paying £1 a head to sit on hard seats.

What made it unique was that all the parts were played by boys; a thirteen year old lad was the principal girl. Of course they were a bit embarrassed, they were real lads with bruised legs. I started as a Sunbeam and ended up as the Dame in Mother Goose. It is hard to evaluate the confidence that gave me and lads like me. When you close a church or chapel you take away an amenity which is hard to replace.

☐ People think that tenants' associations are a new thing but Smith House had one as long ago as the early 1950s. I should know, I was its community queen.

I can't remember exactly how I got the job. Judges who were nothing to do with the estate were brought in and we girls had to parade about and then read

*Gill Cliff*

*Heptonstall 1989*

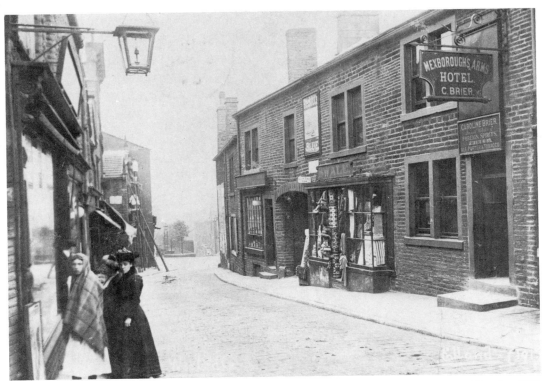

*Westgate, Elland c. 1900*

*Pat, The Tenant's Association Queen*

something. I got the job. One of the neighbours had his nose put out of joint because his daughter wasn't chosen.

On the big day I was dressed in white satin with a royal blue cloak. I made the crown myself using sequins. Then we were paraded round. You didn't do much after that but you were expected to attend social functions.

There was a lot going off. Olde tyme dancing, whist drives, bonfires, we had the lot. They even organised craft sessions in a room at the back of the Astoria. I made a brooch out of plastic. Then there was the pantomime for young people in the Ebenezer Chapel at Bailiff Bridge.

In the end, although people like Mr Donson worked hard, it fizzled out; families moved away, television came along. I lost touch when I got married.

## It's a fairer system

☐   The pre-fabs up Cow Lane showed what could be done if the government thought seriously about better housing. By today's standards maybe they look small, but they were no smaller than the average flat in a tower block.

☐   It was never my intention to live in a pre-fab. Many people, myself included, said they looked like flat-topped hen huts and were scruffy. I had never been inside one, so I had no idea what it would be like inside.

One day a terrific gale hit a row of them and number 22 lost its roof. The bedroom walls were also damaged. At the time, my husband, two year old son and myself lived in a condemned house. A housing officer came round and offered us number 22. My immediate reaction was, I didn't want to live there, but he explained that a new roof had been put on, and the bedroom wall was rebuilt and emulsioned. After a short while I was persuaded to at least go and view it.

When my husband came home from work we set off to look at the "hen hut". We saw a square box with grubby-looking walls. I said, "I'm not going to live there." However, going through the gate, down two steps, into a small garden, we entered a different world. The back door led into a small but compact, fitted kitchen with a gas fridge, a sink, a bench, and a gas cooker and another bench. Underneath the benches were cupboards, one with a vegetable rack. Behind the back door was a broom cupboard, and on the other wall, a cupboard for crockery. In the living room was another fitted cupboard opposite two big corner windows. The small coal fire, I remember, had doors which could be closed for safety at night, or if you went out shopping. In the hall there was the front door at one end and a separate toilet at the other. Left of the hall were two good-sized square bedrooms, again with fitted cupboards. The bathroom contained a wash basin, bath and arched shelves, and, best of all, a heated towel rail.

To say I was delighted with the "hen hut" is putting it mildly. We decided there and then, and within a week we moved in over the Easter weekend.

Looking back, the pre-fab was very easy to run, housework was a joy instead of a chore. Consider the advantages. There were no stairs to climb. From the front door down the steps, we were in a large garden which was just right for hanging out the washing, and for my son and his pals to play at their games.

When the time came for the pre-fabs to be pulled down the tenants were all sorry to leave even though we were to be moved to a new estate. To us the pre-fabs were the ideal accommodation; the only thing they needed to be perfect was a brick casing on the outer walls. I wish even now to be back in our "hen hut", for it housed us during the happiest years of our lives.

☐    If you have a true steel framed house you have difficulty in selling because people round here prefer brick or stone houses. Four years ago we could have bought ours for about £8,000 but our firm declared a lot of redundancies so it didn't seem worth it. One with vacant possession would go for £11,000. The council is pretty decent.

☐    I worked in housing most of my life. In Clifton where I live there are a couple of

*Tarran houses*

43

*Jumples Flats, Mixenden 1985*

small council developments. I think that the smaller units of council housing are good. The bigger the estate is, the bigger the problems. The fill-in estates built by the council have been very satisfactory. When the old lady who lived in a large house in its own grounds in Ash Grove died the council bought the property and put a development up which now houses thirty to forty people. It is these smaller units that have been the most successful from the tenants' point of view. People do move from their own houses to council flats when they are older and find it a problem to heat a house. There are not many private flats in Brighouse and those that exist tend to be luxury flats and of high cost.

There was a housing problem in Brighouse but when Whinney Hill was built, that solved the problem. I think there are about 300 units on Whinney Hill. Municipal ownership can only be good. The Local Authority has to provide a service, private speculators are only into making a profit. Under municipal ownership the expenses are shared, the finances are pooled. This means that if money is needed to do urgent work on an estate all the council tenants are paying towards it. It's a fairer system.

☐ I lived on the fifth floor. The lifts were always breaking down. If the one with odd numbers broke down, I had to go up to the sixth floor and walk down. Needless to say, it was usually my lift that broke.

Talbot House had a lot of old folk, but they've started putting young ones in, I don't agree with them mixing young and old.

☐ They started building our house on Granny Hill Park in 1939. It was a private builder called Lapish's of Brighouse. When the war came they stopped building. After the war they were not building private houses so these houses

44

were completed by Brighouse Council. We moved in when I left the forces in 1949. There were a lot of young families on this estate when it first opened.

My ambition was to have a decent home. We thought about buying a one-up one-down but then decided to go for a council house.

## Ten in a small house, two in a big one

☐   I came over to England after the war. Halroyd's Cotton Mill advertised for workers in my native Austria. I came to Elland on a two year contract at Halroyd's. The contract meant I had to stay at the mill for those two years at least. I met my husband over here, he worked at Lockwood's Dry Cleaning. The mill closed in 1952 but there was plenty of work then. You could finish a job today and start another tomorrow. I think it is harder for youngsters now, though people should strive to better themselves. I like England very much but it is abused and mismanaged. If people never spent more than they earned they'd be happier. We never had two purses, just the one because we trusted one another. When you're in debt happiness flies out of the window.

☐   A lot of houses round Islamabad in places like Lahore and Rawalpindi are really fashionable and elegant. People think of Pakistan and India as a place of villages with little mud huts, of course there is that, but when you think of it, there's a wide variety of houses in Halifax too.

I am very proud of the Piece Hall, all Asians love it, but there are very different parts to Halifax. Some are also elegant, such as the Savile Park area, and therefore very expensive with houses selling at £300,000, but there are still houses which will sell for as little as £12,000.

I am seventeen now and hope to be a

*Piece Hall, Halifax c. 1900*

businessman when I grow up, most Asians do, and that's why we want to be educated. I will be more advanced.

When my parents' generation came over we were in what you might call the houses of desperation, overcrowded housing. Sometimes people would work on day shifts and then swap beds with night shift workers. It was a difficult environment to cope with. We want more, are more individualistic. My bedroom, for instance, is covered in posters of people like Madonna and Michael Jackson, whereas the living room only has pictures of mosques and religious things on the walls. The only things I cannot put on the walls are Moonie posters. They are against our religion. When I get my big house it will contain some things from my English and some from my Pakistani past. The walls will be covered in velvet wall paper and the gardens contain water fountains.

☐ Westhill Park, at the top of Gibbet Street, is a Moslem area with the Central Mosque – Madni, at its centre. The houses were originally built for Crossley's workers. What you notice is that although the windows are hung with bright garlands of artificial flowers there is no attempt to cultivate the gardens.

☐ I was born here and I love it, especially the countryside around Ingleton and the Lakes. My parents have not seen as much as I have although we have relatives in London, Birmingham and Newcastle. The school took me to see a lot of interesting places. I would like a house up there but I would put up with a roof over my head; you cannot do without a roof.

I have a white girlfriend, her family have six bedrooms.

☐ I own my house, three bedrooms. Our family is nine people. I like British houses. I will move again eventually, somewhere bigger.

☐ The Asian population is spread in an odd way in the Calderdale area. In Todmorden, for instance, there is a solidly Asian population in back-to-back housing close to the main street but in Hebden Bridge, a few miles down the valley, there is not one Asian family to my knowledge. There is a ghetto in Westhill but only a sprinkling in other towns. Where I lived previously, in Mirfield, there were hardly any Asians but Dewsbury and Batley have big populations.

☐ I have read somewhere that Halifax has one of the oldest Asian populations in the country; that some mill owners, as early as 1850, sent to India for workers.

☐ Local estate agents hide their racism with phrases like, "You know it's beyond Queen's Road" or by dropping their voice and saying, "It's close to a Pakistani area." I said to one, "I'm not sure I want to buy a house from a racist."

☐ We all live at home, we share a bedroom with a sister. Our dream house? I'd like a semi-detached, with everything matching in the rooms, or a cottage on a country lane or an apartment with a balcony and a view.

☐ My mother-in-law is Polish and the house is filled with crucifixes and coloured runners which go along the tops of furniture. The Catholicism dominates the house to the extent that when her first grandchild was born she painted a garish picture of Jesus and his bleeding side for the child's bedroom. Before it went up she took it to the priest to have it blessed.

☐ I live in Rawalpindi; I am staying with my daughter here till September. I have children in Pakistan and children here – it is a big problem. The main difference between houses in Pakistan and houses in Britain is the weather. The young people are all right but the cold in these houses is a problem for us.

*Gibbet Lane 1989*

In Pakistan we have big houses and small houses same as here — more money, more comfort. Ten people in a small house, two rich people in a big one. It's the same problem everywhere.

☐ My taste's very different from my dad's. He's old-fashioned, he likes really dark colours, I like bright colours — not too bright, I wouldn't do a bedroom in orange or yellow or anything.

My parents own their house. I'll buy a house when I'm older. It's not difficult — if you get a good job you can get a mortgage. Two of us are at college — we'll get jobs, no problems.

When will I move from my parents to a place of my own? If it was up to me I'd do it now, but it isn't up to me. I'll probably move out when I get married when I'm 24 or 25. Who will choose where I go? I will. Well, if I marry someone from Britain he'll be allowed to help choose but if my husband is in Pakistan I'd do it. I'll know

more about it than he will. I'll just say, "This is good for you, love."

## Women should design houses

☐ I sometimes think that the people who design council houses have no knowledge of the lives of people who live in them. When you have my job you are like an agony aunt. One of the single parents was only sixteen. She was nice but was drifting from fella to fella. Someone like me could have relied on their family to help out but she was alone. Even keeping her flat clean was hard, cleaning materials aren't cheap. It's not like my gran's time when all you needed was carbolic soap and elbow grease to wash down stone flags.

This lass's rooms had really big windows so she needed double lengths of curtaining. I got mine as seconds for smaller windows but that was £17. Hers cost £30 minimum and then there was £24 for net curtains. There was not much change out of £60. After that there was carpeting. The hall in this house where they had put a single mother was 21 feet by 13 feet. Think of the cost. It was like putting a cat in a mansion.

When this estate was built there were couples with a husband and wife both in work. Then you could have little gardens but now with all this unemployment it's a different world.

☐    The drying area is too far away with our place. By the time you get round if it's raining your clothes are wet again, so we have two lines up inside the house and a clothes horse.

☐    The bathroom in our old council house was tiny. They must have put the bath in first and then built round it. You had to stand up in the bath to get dried. Sixty years ago council housing was well designed. I don't think they're up to much these days.

When I lived in Mixy Court we had underfloor heating from vents. It was a dry heat and you always had a sore throat. I would have preferred central heating. If I could have made structural changes I would have put in a serving hatch between the kitchen and living room. The kitchen was too small to eat in. I would also put fitted wardrobes in, a shower as well as a bath, and box in electric and gas meters better. You daren't do anything yourself, though, or else the council would change it all back and send you the bill.

☐    As a council tenant you need permission to make alterations. When you move out you have to leave the improvements behind; if the council doesn't like what you did you have to restore it to its original state.

☐    You can tell it was a man who designed council houses. A woman can see a lot of faults in the design of them. They should have had a woman around to put her spoke in at the time. For instance,

*West Vale School c. 1921*

*The Tenants Association Gala c. 1950*

when they design new council houses they should make much bigger kitchens and put more electric points in and have them higher up the wall to save bending all the time.

☐ It was beautifully designed, a lovely council house in Ovenden. We got the sun in the kitchen in the morning and then in the living room in the afternoon. There is nothing I'd have done to change it.

## The house of your dreams

☐ They couldn't build the type of kitchen I want into a council house. I want real beams, a low ceiling and all the pans out on the wall like they did in very old farmhouses. I'm fed up rooting for pans in the cupboards. Have you ever noticed that although there is plenty of cupboard space in council houses it's always in the wrong place? With all that I would get down to some serious cooking.

I don't cook too much meat these days. When I worked at a butcher's we would sometimes get lambs in, so recently killed that their little hearts were still warm. That put me off. My boy friend also cooks so we are into lasagna, chilli-con-carne, savoury pancakes, and spaghetti dishes.

☐ When we were first married my husband designed a settee with leather cushions to fit over the bath in the kitchen. He was an engineer and good at making things like that.

☐ I live in Boothtown in two terraced houses that have been knocked into one. Because I have spina bifida I have special design requirements. There is a ramp up to the front door, wider doorways and an adapted bathroom. The house has its limitations and I have difficulties. I have to go in forwards and reverse to come out of the bathroom, and can only just squeeze into the kitchen. It doesn't make it easier when grant applications and planning permission get turned down. My list of design essentials for a new house would include a wide bathroom, with moulded seating in the bath and easy operated pulley system, a wide kitchen and generally enough room for me to turn round in my chair without difficulty.

☐ I am living in a council house now, but I've never felt settled. I am waiting for my own house in Ireland to be sold so I can use the money for a deposit on a house. I would like a stone cottage with some character. Modern houses are such boxes. The picture I have in mind is something slightly modern but old in style. The decor would be co-ordinated, with pelmets over the windows and Austrian blinds, boards on the wall, wooden floors with rugs thrown on them. I want a through-room so I don't have to move from one room to another and there's not the bother of shutting doors. I suppose I might as well dream here as in bed.

☐ I'd like an old-fashioned house, 500 years old, with black and white wood. Not all old-fashioned — inside you'd need a video, a cooker, all modern things — but old on the outside. I live at home but I'd like to live with a friend. My dad could easily afford that but he wouldn't want to, he wants me at home.

☐ I'd like a Tudor house, there's one for sale up near Hipperholme now, right old-fashioned outside. I'll buy a house, not rent, but it won't be for ages yet. I'll finish college first then I'll think about it.

☐ People ask, "If you could design the house of your dreams what would it be like?" I used to live in a one-up one-down in Halifax so the house of my dreams is something like the terraced house I live in now; three bedrooms, a very big kitchen, and what I call The Room, high ceilings and plenty of space. My son has a town house, though for me it looks like a terraced house.

*Towngate, Northowram*

*The bridge below the hole in the sky, Elland*

☐ Today people of my age, I'm twenty four, think in terms of things. A tumble dryer, automatic washing machine, microwave oven and dish washer are seen as essential. If you haven't got a video people will say, "Haven't you got that??" and mean, "You must be really poor."

☐ A few years ago everyone went in for the red and white kitchens. Towels, cupboards, wall-mounted tin openers, meat knives, kettles — everything in red and white. Before that it was pine kitchens; ceilings, walls, everything pine or paper that looked like pine, and earlier still it was flush doors. Now people tear those off and sand down to the pine.

☐ We feel cut off since they built the motorway. They knocked a lot of council houses down to build the motorway. To get into Elland now you have to go over the motorway bridge. Folk don't like going over motorways in high winds to do their shopping. It used to be a pleasant walk into town.

☐ I think that the newer council estates are a lot better. Valley View Park is nice and the houses are well designed but in my opinion all council estates should be smaller and there should be greater variety.

Red brick houses make me think of council houses. I've known people who won't buy a house because it's built of red brick. It's not because they think the houses are worse, it's just a case of snobbery.

☐ When I worked in housing we used to get people in the office and they would pester and pressure us to try and get a house they wanted. This would happen especially when new property was being built by the council. Some people would have breakfast, dinner and tea with us in the offices. The funny thing is that they would have got the house they wanted if they hadn't pressured us but it was no use telling them.

□   A lot have through-lounges these days. I couldn't do with one. You pay enough on gas and electricity bills without heating all that extra space.

I wouldn't want a bedsit, living and sleeping in the same room isn't healthy. Central heating is a bit unhealthy as well. I like a cold bedroom. Before I moved into my old folks' flat I used to leave my bedroom window open all the time. I've been known to clear snow up in the bedroom before now.

□   We have got a through-lounge, two rooms knocked through, so we're getting the use of the room and there's no waste of space. We don't need a dining room since our meal times are different and we only sit down together for Saturday tea and Sunday lunch. Having space is important. My parents' living room was very small. The other room was the kitchen. When my husband and I lived with them, we had no privacy and it was unthinkable for us to go up to our room. We would all get on top of each other sometimes, especially once there was a baby.

□   I've lived in a council house for thirty six years. When mine was built it was very modern but they haven't kept up as well as they should. We don't have central heating, just a gas fire in the front room and cold bedrooms. Mind you, a lot who have central heating don't use it, they say it's a dry heat. I'd definitely like double glazing though.

□   I live in a multi-storey flat in Westbrook Court. There's seventeen floors with six flats on each floor and I live on the fifth floor. It's homely enough if you're in your sixties, but for a young lass like me it's no good. The older people have bingo days and meet up in each other's flats and they also have the community room. They all talk to me, and ask me for sweets sometimes because I work up at Mackintosh's. However, I only know the names of the people on my floor but upwards to floor seventeen I don't know anyone. It's like living in a prison — you get locked in and speak to no-one.

I used to live in Illingworth, in a maisonette down Fieldhead Lane. When Wimpey started building a new estate all the old houses were pulled down and we were all moved into the multi-storeys. I preferred the maisonette but I still like to keep my flat smart. I paint and decorate, but if it was my own I'd do far more. However, I like to think it will be nice for when I leave and the next people come in.

Even though I don't see many people, I often feel I'm being watched. The other tenants notice who you bring back and it all goes down on your point system. Each tenant gets points every year and it all depends on whether you've caused any bother or come back drunk or anything like that. At the moment I've got 97 points out of 100 and I want to keep it that way, because if you've got a good record you'll get another place.

I think council housing is a good thing because people always need homes. However, if I was a council fella I'd knock down the multi-storeys and build streets. My dream is a house with a garden, and in a street you see your neighbours day to day. The problem at the moment is that there are some very lonely people cooped up in those multi-storeys.

□   I've experienced homelessness in the past, so a dream home to me is four walls and a roof over my head. At present I'm stuck in bedsitland. I've lived in one after another for a number of years. It can be really depressing; you need to decorate them brightly. I paint, so I put my own work up. Bedsits are invariably found in grotty rundown areas, old listed buildings owned by private landlords who for the most part don't care as long as they're creaming off the grant monies and tax allowances.

*Corn Market, Halifax*

One of the saddest things about housing in this area is the lack of it. The council is selling off and turning properties into offices. It's surprising how many homeless people there are around here. More money should be put into house building instead of road building. Somewhere to live is more important than how quickly you can get to work. I once lived in a squat where we daubed "Houses not roads" on the front door, so that everybody driving to work could see it. A few months afterwards they knocked the house down to widen the road.

## Measure Imperial and get metric

☐    The design is appalling and it wouldn't be tolerated in a private house. It would cost next to nothing to put a box round the electricity meter but no, it has to hang suspended from the wall above the hall doorway. The heating unit is the same. It just hangs there.

☐    My main complaint about the council is money wasting. They should make sure they get their money's worth from outside contractors. Some are real cowboys. They came to fit new windows, measured Imperial but metric arrived. They had to rebate the frames to make them fit. I have three window ledges now and they're a devil to paint. There are all sorts of cases, leaking pipes put down as condensation, gates that don't fit the gate holes. My niece had a new bath put in and they forgot to connect the outlet pipe to the drainage.

The standard of some of the workmanship is very slapdash. They said all the doors had to be painted. One painter painted over some old paint that was already blistered, nobody with any sense would do that. I could have stood across the street with a long stick and done a better job.

They don't monitor work as well as they should, they should have more rigorous standards and inspectors. Work should be surveyed on completion, and if it didn't come up to scratch they wouldn't get paid.

The last time they "modernised" inside, all I gained was a new bath and toilet, and new windows which only let as much light in as the others. It cost me a fortune, they took my old cupboards out. I had to buy a new carpet to cover the gap and redecorate the rooms.

One thing about council houses, there's always some coming empty, but if they keep selling them there won't be any left.

☐    When we got to the new house there was no gate or fence so I went to the council for them. They said, "Fill in these forms" so I did but nothing happened. For a time, I forgot all about it but when I got round to looking into it again I found that they had been cutting back. Now they would supply and bed in the gate post, but not supply the gate. More central government cutbacks and we have got to the position that the council will provide the post if I bed it in.

☐    I have got an insurance policy and I expect work to be done on my house if things go wrong. I think it should be the same for council tenants, considering the amount of rent they have to pay. In fact, I think that rents should be lowered and people should be encouraged to look after the house themselves with the extra money. This would make people more responsible for their own properties. I'm not over-houseproud, though, for me furniture is to sit on, not to look at.

I don't think it's fair putting people in those multi-storey blocks of flats. The people who designed these properties ought to be made to live in them.

☐    What strikes you in this area as an outsider is the beauty of buildings and the fact that there is such a variety. The stone is beautiful and there are strong architectural features like mullion windows. On top of that there are the vistas such as the ones you get around Rishworth, Elland and Hebden Bridge.

☐ Now a lot of people have bought their council houses. They've put double-glazing in and added new porches. They look smashing but you need a grant. I was too old when they offered mine for sale so I didn't bother.

☐ I sold my house last year and moved to a council house on Westgate. I used to do all the house maintenance but as I'm getting on a bit now, I can't do it any more. I begrudge paying a builder £10 an hour for sitting round drinking tea.

☐ Council houses were built to standards. It took much longer for reasonable sanitation to reach a lot of the older private rented properties. When I was a girl we had no bathroom, just a tin bath, and an outside toilet to share between four houses. Where I lived there were tub toilets emptied by men with a horse and cart. Farmers used to buy the soil. As a girl I had to scrub the white seats. It was heaven when we got a water closet; I kept pulling the chain. That was when I was about eighteen. Different areas got theirs later. It was 1952 before Booth got water toilets and proper sewers.

How many people do you think went upstairs with a bucket and a ladling can with water to empty the you-know-what? One! That was my job!

☐ We had an iron fireplace, so we used to fill the copper at the side, and with a ladling can we took the water out of the side boiler and put it into a tin bath. We hadn't water in the cellar, so my husband used to have to carry the bath up and put it in front of the fire. My grandchildren think it sounds awful, but it was lovely.

☐ One end of the tin bath was called the shed. When you were little you had your bath in front of the fire but when you were bigger you had to go down to the cellar. In those days you had to light the washing boiler to heat your bath water. Some houses had their own toilet, some had to

*Charabanc trip c. 1925*

55

*Council housing, Morland View, Sowerby*

share. Some even had to go to the bottom of the street to the toilet. Other toilets were in rows and you had a key to lock them up. Toilets were mostly at the bottom of yards and they used to freeze up in winter.

☐ There were three of us living on Moorfield Street in a four storey house, attic, bedroom, room and cellar kitchen. We had some steps going down to the cellar kitchen and at the bottom on the right hand side was the old toilet. Once every three weeks we had to do our share on Saturday morning of yellow-stoning those steps. I donkey-stoned the front and only got out of it if it was raining. There were back-to-back houses on Moorfield Street; and where we lived, on Savile Park Terrace, the back came up to some houses they built in Ingram Street. They've modernised them now and they're in a sort of mews.

☐ I'll tell you what we had in one kitchen that used to fascinate me. We had a set pan with a fire underneath; a great big copper with a great wooden lid on top. You used to fill it with water and put the fire in the little grate. This had to be kept going but it would boil clothes beautifully. Everything you wanted went into the set pan. If it was a rainy day, we used what we called winter hedges. They were clothes horses, really, but no one called them that. I was taught to iron when I was very young. I was at Parkinson Lane School.

We had a flat iron to begin with, but that was a bit of a nuisance. You had to put it on a stand and be careful with it. Then we progressed to a huge charcoal iron. It had an opening at the back for the charcoal. I loved that because the charcoal looked like old bobbins. Eventually you got it all red hot, and then you had to keep that going. It was lovely how hot it got. It had a metal casing on the bottom so it didn't burn your clothes. As a young girl I used to do the handkerchiefs when I came home and gradually I was promoted to doing the towels. I loved that but really preferred filling the iron up.

☐ Our council house door fell off one day and I got pinned underneath it. My neighbour came running and rescued me. He told me not to open it again as the hinges had gone but to get straight down to the council. Well, I went down and told them. In the end I got sick of going round the door so I got a joiner in to fix it. Three years later the council joiner came and knocked on the door, "I've come to fix your door." I couldn't even remember it, it was that long ago.

A few years later a patch of plaster fell out from under the lounge window. I thought, I'm not going to get caught again. I went down to the housing and gave them a right roasting. Blow me, two days later a lorry turned up at our house with four workmen. They were ready to get stuck into a major job. I was a bit embarrassed when I showed them the little patch of plaster missing in the lounge.

☐ We moved out of our own house because they knocked it down. We got a council house and decorated it throughout, we got it looking lovely. Then my husband died. They moved us out and shoved us in the multi-storeys in Mixenden. I couldn't live there. You were trapped. Nowhere for the kids to play, nowhere to do the washing – we used to dry the clothes in the airing cupboard.

☐ We bought our one bedroomed back-to-back house in 1964 for £350. We bought it mainly to move into Halifax to look for somewhere better. We had to move when the council demolished it. The compensation didn't give us enough to buy another home.

☐ It was a lot of money to us then but we didn't want a council house so we paid £500 for a back-to-back. They're going for

*Central car park, Elland*

*Mixenden Parents Resource Centre 1989*

£13,000 now, everybody wants them. A woman near us has just paid £2,000 for new doors and windows. They've all been made nice. There used to be one room down and two bedrooms, but the second bedroom we turned into a bathroom and inside toilet. A lot have converted their attics and put dormer windows in, they make grand warm rooms. I'm glad we bought it when we did, when you look at the rent on council houses – and you're beholden to the council as well.

## Mixenden folk don't mix

☐  When you look down on Mixenden you have got to admit that it is terrific, really beautiful. It has been lifted dramatically in the last few years. The have fenced the gardens, pebbledashed the fronts of the houses and put on new roofs. The council is realising that you can't go on doing patch-up jobs, you've got to think big.

☐  A lot of folk in Mixenden don't mix. It's split into five different parts: the village that's the original Mixenden, Hambleton, Stanningley and Woodbrook – that's a nice part, so people buy the houses there – then there's Dodgeholme, that's the flats.

I love my house, but I'd like to pick it up and put it somewhere else.

☐  I left home at nineteen because I wanted to live with my boyfriend. We lived at Mixenden Court on the tenth floor of fifteen.

We split up when I was pregnant and I moved back home. I told the council I wanted another place because I was expecting. They kept me waiting until the last minute. The baby was due in March and I got the keys on 18th February. They gave me a two-bedroomed place on Hambleton Court in Mixenden. Rainwater came up through the floorboards and eventually I got a note from the doctor to say it was detrimental to my little girl's health. After a lot of arguments I got a flat on Clough Bank, also in Mixenden.

☐ The houses on Clough Bank have been completely shelled, stripped down to the bricks, roofs taken off and replaced. They were refurbished with new bathrooms, new plaster, new double glazing. They've made nice houses but some people still aren't looking after them.

☐ There are a lot of good folk in Mixenden, a lot of intelligent people as well. People should consider that before they call us names.

☐ The *Halifax Courier* gives a terrible impression of Mixenden. If there's a mouse seen in a window here it makes the headlines in that paper even if it is a pet mouse. But the truth is that Mixenden is a lovely area. I've lived here twenty years and wouldn't want to live anywhere else. The scenery is lovely and it's peaceful. When you tell people you're from Mixenden they turn their noses up, where do they get their information? It can only be from papers and such like.

☐ We got known as a problem family area. That's just lumping together and categorising. The majority of people here don't have problems but they get called. They're perfectly happy with their lot, that's all. Council officials come round branding us. They say, "All of these single parent families are having their boyfriends in", as though that is a crime. My flat was spotlessly clean, but because I am a one parent family on income support I'm regarded as a problem. The real problems are broken down lifts, design faults, lack of communal facilities and children's play areas.

Those high-rise flats were ten years out of date when they were built. Installing security cameras in the entrance hall doesn't stop people from coming in. You hear echoes and bangings all the time in flats, so one more broken door or window doesn't mean anything. The whole design is a paradise for burglars. It is the design that is breeding crime.

☐ Some teachers' expectations of Mixy kids leave a lot to be desired. I call it Mixendenitis — lumping Mixy people together as no hopers. We haven't got the support we need, or, for that matter, the resources.

☐ Some reckon that they put all the bad families on council estates in Mixenden. It's not true. My sister needed a house fast, her husband had just come out of the forces after nine years. He was unemployed so they had to take what they were given. The place has a bad reputation and all the people who live there get tarred with the same brush. Some of the houses and gardens are really nice and well cared for. On the other hand others use their gardens for dismantling cars and their gardens look more like junk yards. I don't know how that problem could be solved, these people have to live somewhere.

☐ The Parents' Resource Centre was set up for mums and dads on the Mixenden Estate. Sadly, Mixenden has had a bad press but we try to get positive images into print about the estate so that residents don't think they live in some dead end. People around here already feel they are peripheral to what's going on; Halifax is an expensive bus ride away. It is true there is an element of vandalism and high unemployment, but we hope to show there is more to Mixenden. We operate an open door policy at the centre — the only thing we ask is that there is no violence in the centre.

☐ A credit union was set up in Mixenden to combat loan sharks and the blacklist. A lot of people were taking out loans with loan sharks because they couldn't get credit. Many couldn't get credit due to being blacklisted by banks.

One road in particular gained a reputation for poor credit, at times this was undeserved. Whole streets, not just people, were blacklisted which meant that if the previous tenant was a bad debtor, you were automatically regarded as a bad payer too.

We were lucky to have the help of the Credit Union Development Officer from Bradford but when Bradford said he could no longer work in Calderdale we resorted to constant lobbying and managed to get a short term development officer for Calderdale.

The idea of the Credit Union is to encourage thrift. The member has to prove that s/he can put money aside each week before being allowed a loan.

☐ Various loan companies started coming round knocking on doors asking if people required a loan. Some reps already had the money in their hands, waving the notes. Repayments were up to forty per cent. A lot of these people operated under the name of reputable companies but they were nothing more than gangsters in suits and ties, loan sharks. The Credit Union is set up to fight them, irrespective of whether the loans are coming from reputable companies or shady individuals.

The Credit Union was originally set up in the Parents' Resource Centre in 1986 and ran for one year before it folded. It then restarted in June 1987 in the Church of the Holy Nativity. Now it is no longer run by a group of friends but is a full legal body.

We have forty to fifty members in Mixenden with an account at Mixenden Post Office and one at the Halifax Building Society. In my opinion I think we should be looking for organisations to invest in who don't have shady connections. We don't want South African companies for example.

☐ After the war there were severe shortages. I wanted an Acme washing machine so we asked at the Co-op. The

*Ackroyden 1850s model housing*

Gill Cliff

*Model housing 1989*

manager ushered us upstairs and there, under a sheet, were two machines. He asked us if we would be paying cash or wanting hire purchase. We said, "Cash" and got it. Today they would prefer it the other way.

☐ One thing I don't like about Mixenden is all the dogs, running wild and messing everywhere. They are also dangerous, jumping up at the children. Things are made worse because most of the gardens are designed open plan. I have never seen a dog warden round here. Don't get me wrong, I don't dislike dogs. I've got one myself.

☐ I've lived in Mixenden all my life and wouldn't want to move away. I got my own first house here at sixteen when I got married and I hope eventually to buy one here. I moved out once but moved back. I like being near my family; it's important to be close to your relatives.

You hear stories about towns where they are putting plastic cows up for people to look at. I can look out of my window and see real ones. There's some lovely walks on the moors and by the reservoir, you can take a picnic and enjoy the fresh air, you can't beat it.

## Women trapped at home

☐ I used to do homework or outwork, as some call it. Women with small children usually do it when they can't get out to work in factories. Stuff is sent out and handled by a middleman. We used to make Christmas crackers. My husband helped me because he was unemployed as well.

We sat up all night sometimes, eighty to ninety hours per week, for between fifteen and eighteen pounds. That works out at about 20p an hour. We did it to pay the bills but sitting up all the time burning

61

electricity hardly made it worth it. When they got a rush order, the man would come and say something like, "I need six hundred extra boxes by the end of the weekend." We stopped up all Saturday and Sunday night for an extra £2 bonus. It was dangerous as well, having your front room packed with inflammable stuff.

Most outwork is very repetitive, simple work. To speed things up, one of our neighbours invented a machine to make it easier and quicker. We usually did crackers, but other folk do cards into boxes, light fittings, pegs, landing platforms for budgies, mopheads, small assembly and packing work. Some of the work is highly skilled. Some women are paid £4 to make wool sweaters with complicated patterns which are then sold in London. The labels read *Hand knitted in Yorkshire*. They sell for over £100 in London.

A lot of people are afraid to come forward in case they are shopped and get in trouble with the DHSS. It's wrong what some firms are doing. A cousin of mine worked in a factory under one name in the morning and another in the afternoon. In the end I decided to jack it in and see if I could do something about it. I went to a conference in Bradford organised by the West Yorkshire Home Working Group and people from the Low Pay Unit. Up till then I thought that only me and another girl from Mixenden were doing it but there were people from all over the country. There are a lot of Asian women involved.

From that point I decided to hold my own meetings and leafleted the whole estate, 1,700 houses. Only eleven people turned up at the first meeting but we continue to meet regularly.

After that I went to the Manchester Conference organised by the European Network of Women. We had our photographs taken in the Emily Pankhurst Memorial Room and I was chosen to go to Brussels. I spoke at the European Parliament and my words were translated into nine languages.

*Mill girls, Sowerby Bridge 1907*

It seems that economic pressures are the primary reason for women to accept homework at low rates of pay. Their circumstances also deter them from uniting to obtain better conditions. The employer simply drops them at the first whisper of discontent, making up any production shortfall by employing someone else or increasing pressure on other workers. The situation is not dissimilar to that existing when women and children worked in the mines. Individual protest led to economic extinction and attempts at unity were ruthlessly crushed. It required legislation then, as now, to remedy this situation.

I visited Brussels in November 1988 for a tribunal on women's poverty along with other women from the UK. It was an experience never to be forgotten. There were 170 women there from every member state of the EEC. The event was organised by the European Network of Women (ENOW) to draw attention to the fact that it is women who bear the burden of poverty. I was chosen as one of ten women to give evidence of women living in poverty in the UK to the European Parliament.

I spoke of the exploitation of women trapped at home, and in particular those doing outwork. Other women spoke of a range of problems women face; lack of employment and lack of benefit, lack of adequate housing and lack of childcare facilities, domestic violence and lack of medical care.

Women at the meeting stated clearly that their poverty came not just from a lack of income. The poor are worse off in comparison with the rest of the population, not only in income but also in their long term financial and life prospects and their access to real opportunities to participate in, and influence, change.

Within the total EEC population of 320 million, there are an estimated 44 million poor people, the majority of them women.

ENOW hopes they have influenced the European Parliament to develop a programme to combat poverty, particularly with reference to women, as an integral part of the development of a single European Community in 1992.

☐ There is only one childminder in Mixenden and she can take only two kids in because she's already a foster mother. Women are trapped in their homes because there's no-one to look after their children. A lot of women won't become childminders because of the regulations which are very strict.

☐ I came from Dublin in April 1987 because my husband could not find work. We spent three and a half months in London in bed and breakfast accommodation that cost the authorities £35 a night. My husband tried his best to find work but was turned away because he couldn't supply a steady address. My husband's aunt lives in Ovenden so we came up here. After three weeks we got a place in Mixenden in Balkram Road. The trouble is, we have come from a place where there was work and nowhere to live, to a place where there is somewhere to live and no work.

☐ You ask what housing provision is based on in the late 1980s. I'll tell you: Brass, brass and persecution.

## Hebden — put to the test by "off-comers"

☐ Hebden's characterisation as a town where the ethnic skirts sweep the pavements is simplified. More and more, it's considered a place for yuppies. There are a lot of media people, artists and writers. Perhaps people have always come to a place like Hebden to get away from it all but there are also people with 2.4 children living very conventional lives.

☐ For me Hebden's setting amongst the sometimes beautiful, sometimes grim

*Hebden Bridge 1986*

Pennine Hills was certainly part of its attraction but it was the people too, the town had an air of aliveness that I had been missing.

In 1986 Hebden house prices were already quite high. Our previous house bought two years earlier in a South Yorkshire pit village had cost just £8,500 and it had central heating. In Hebden we paid £23,000 for a terraced house with a derelict underdwelling, ripe for conversion. When we split up some time later our joint house sold for £42,000. There was no need to advertise, people were queuing up to buy. I know that three months after we sold the value of the house had reached £60,000. The proceeds paid for my small back-to-back which came to £28,000 and one at £7,000 in Todmorden.

Some people are now thinking of selling up and moving to Todmorden. It's so much cheaper. In Hebden there is a shortage of the type of family housing people want and a shortage of building land. The developers are busy building wherever they are allowed to, throwing up modern brick and timber prefabs almost overnight. They sell before they are finished and they are expensive for what they are. I suppose they could be worse, the trouble is they are all exactly alike and no-one knows how long they will last. Many of the old houses here have damp, being on the hillside, but they are solid and they've lasted. What's more important they have character.

Hebden is full of character. People round here have always had character, sorely put to the test when "oft-comers" flood the place and house prices soar so that their children can't afford to live here anymore. Councils starved of money can no longer step in to provide good cheap housing for the young people.

The early influx of "oft-comers" was poor, attracted by the beauty of the place, maybe the tolerance, certainly the cheap housing. The local population was dwindling then in the sixties. Now visitors invade Hebden on weekends and bank holidays. They stand outside Watson's the baker's, saying, "What a lovely shop." Really they're missing the point. To get to the lovely places you have to get your boots on and make a bit of an effort.

I suppose it's the same everywhere but there are those of us who do not want to live in a goldfish bowl. No wonder some of us are talking of moving four miles up the road to Todmorden.

## Prices go sky high

☐   My daughter and a friend bought a two bedroom flat in May 1989 for £67,000. It was in a street of terraced housing and maisonettes — flats with their own front door — in what she describes as a "very much working class district of London's East End." If she wants to live in the south it's logical to buy because people in her job

— she takes home £150 a week — will spend about £60 a week rent.

☐   I moved to a little cottage in Northowram to be near my daughter. When my husband and I set up home 55 years ago we rented off Dempster's at Elland. It was tied accommodation. About 26 years ago when my husband moved on we bought our own house. It was a three bedroom terraced house with no bathroom and it cost about £1,200. We needed the rooms for our son and daughter but after they left home we converted one of the bedrooms into a bathroom. I don't know how young people can manage to buy at today's prices; I couldn't sleep if I knew I had to pay off a £60,000 mortgage.

☐   We bought our house 12 months ago before the prices went sky high. We wanted one of the old stone houses because they are built far more strongly. New houses just seem to get thrown together.

*Burnley Road, Todmorden 1919*

*Fenton Street Gang c. 1929*

*Council house improvements 1989*

We have everything close by: a park, a school, a supermarket, which is not too brilliant but handy when you run out of something.

Halifax is made up of lots of different areas and people tend to stick with people from their own estate. It's the estates which create the communities.

☐ My first house was an old terraced cottage in Denholme. I found exactly what I had been looking for, it had a good feel about it. It's odd but my taste seems to be the opposite of my parents'. I prefer old furniture and Victorian ornaments, I treasure my china plates and a Victorian ginger jar. I set up house on my own, so the rise in interest rates affected me badly. Mind, selling the cottage was no problem. I'm now looking for a property with a garden big enough for my four dogs, so I suppose it will have to be a modern semi.

☐ Our first house was one of the old mill terraced houses but we wanted a garden for the dog and we were lucky enough to find a cheap semi in a residential area in Greetland. We made a few bob on selling our first house. We were quite emotionally attached to this house. I would have loved to take the bathroom with me, it was spacious with a lovely high window.

We see our present house as an investment. It's only two-bedroomed and now we're looking for a three-bedroomed semi in the same area. Hopefully, we'll again find something rundown which needs doing up. My first priority will be to redecorate. It feels unclean until we've done it.

☐ The trouble with the term yuppies is that it is used loosely to describe almost any comers-in. Okay, there are people with Suzuki four wheel drive cars up in the hill farms but the majority of people who come out here are not upwardly mobile, just people who want their children to live in beautiful surroundings and go to reasonable state schools.

## The devil you know

□ The problem for the future will be that we will not be able to improve an estate in a comprehensive way. At the moment, if you want to gut a number of houses, twenty or thirty, then you can do it using capital monies. Take the Ovenden development. These houses have been up for forty years, and to improve them in a comprehensive way you have to chip off the plaster and get back to the skeleton of the house. It's no use doing less. That done, you can put in double glazing, insulation, rewiring, the lot. It will cost in the region of £16,000 per house.

These Ovenden houses are probably the last houses which will get this treatment. From now on we will have to finance improvement out of revenue. This will mean that the rents will go up towards what is termed an "economic rent".

□ When property improvement takes place there is a slight rise in rents, this is not because of the improvement but because of additional amenities like radiators. In real terms this means that a three-bedroomed house costs about £32 a week rather than the £27 it costs now. You also have to remember that about seventy five percent of the people up here are on some form of benefit because of retirement or unemployment.

□ After an improvement the tenant has three options; to return to the improved house, to retain the house which has been provided while the improvement has taken place, or take another council property. Calderdale is unusual in offering so much. Many councils take this opportunity to direct people on to more appropriate housing.

The tenant also has the right to buy.

*Vernacular architecture — Towngate, Northowram*

*Modern housing in the vernacular tradition 1988*

One of the houses up Ovenden, for instance, three-bedroomed, recently improved, overlooking the valley, might be valued at £25,000 but with 60% discount for forty years' residency this could be reduced to £15,000.

☐ The rent on my council house went up because it had a view — that's what they told me — so I decided to buy. The mortgage is actually less than the rent. It's a council mortgage and I got a rebate for living in council property for more than twenty years. The way I see it there was very little return for the rent. Mind, it wasn't the Council's fault, it was the Government's. The rise in interest rates has slowed down my paying off because more of the money goes to cover the interest.

☐ We could have bought our council house for about two grand but all the family are grown up and we are quite happy in our corporation flat in Halifax.

☐ My first job was as a packer in the mill, that was in 1968 when it was easy to get a job, but four years later I got redundancy. I was out of work for six months before the Job Centre got me attached to Operation Eyesore. We were to tidy up Honeybone Square and Hollywell Green, with a bit of landscaping and turfing; putting in rose beds, that sort of thing.

Generally people appreciate what you do but there is always that sort of vandal who immediately destroys your effort. Benches get thrown into the pond, trees get ripped out. At first you are annoyed but as time goes on you get used to it and think, "It's the same every year." The public rarely fight back.

When I had been a labourer gardener for thirteen years they sent me off to Huddersfield Tech to do a course. Machine maintenance, bedding out, pruning, chemicals; I did the lot. Mind, I didn't learn too much – I had been doing the job for thirteen years.

☐ One good thing the old Borough Council did was to introduce smoke control. It was very progressive on that front. The banishing of smoke ran hand in hand with the decline of the textile industry and therefore of mill chimneys. It did help immensely to make the area "greener". I read in the paper the other day that Halifax lies second only to Exeter as the most desirable medium sized town in this country.

The Tories try to trick people into owning their own place, but it's nothing more than dangling the carrot in front of donkeys. Look at the number of people who have been thrown out of their homes in the last few years for non-repayment of mortgages, especially since the interest rates went up. They claim that council house tenants are not in control of their own destiny because their homes are owned by the council, but how can you be in control of your own destiny when you're indebted to the Government's whim?

☐ The rise in interest rates made our mortgage jump from £98 by nearly £40, it's a great worry.

☐ I'd rather be under the council, I'll say one thing for them, they've looked after us better than private landlords would.

People should be allowed to buy council houses if they want to but it's running down the stock. I would have bought mine if it had been a semi but it's in a row.

☐ We had no money to buy our own house so we were glad of a council house. If you have no option you're glad of it. We had a three-bedroomed house in Stony Lane but when the kids grew up and moved away, it was too big. My husband had a heart complaint and the stairs became a struggle so we moved to a bungalow in Lightcliffe.

I don't want to be under a private landlord again, we couldn't get anything done. If this Government would allow more money to do repairs the houses would be good.

There's talk of private landlords taking over council houses. Perish the thought. There are old people round us and they're frightened of being turfed out by a private landlord. The council is the devil you know.

## The land under that house is mine

☐ We started off in a one-up one-down cottage. They were only fifty one shillings a week after the war. We had a couple of kids and we were struggling for room. We applied and I was surprised when it was only a matter of weeks before we had got a three-bedroomed house. It was the end of a terrace, the kids loved it.

They were handy, the one-up one-down cottages. They gave you a start when you got married. There's not many of them left now.

☐ My mother came from the Stragg Road area of Halifax. They were quite poor, in fact the kitchen was in a cupboard, but after they got married Dad put £20 down on a £300 house. After he had bought the land Mum persuaded him to back down. She would not owe money. That wasn't uncommon in those days. They paid 3/4d a week for their council house.

I know it was like that because when he would take me for a walk as a child and we would go past the house he would say, "The bit of land under that house is mine."

☐ I was brought up on a farm. I moved into a private house when I got married and it seemed like living in a doll's house. I'm still living in that house 44 years later – it was my first house and I hope it will be my last.

We bought it when my husband was in the forces. It was difficult to get a loan, because people were worried that if he got killed I'd be left with no way of paying them back.

We've done all sorts to it in the last 44 years — turned two bedrooms into three, built a sun lounge and the cellar is as nice to live in as any other room now.

Nearly every other house in the street has had new people in it and I've watched them come and go. Lots of young couples who aren't married move in and out and they seem to work by day and live by night. They live differently to us in two ways. They seem to buy everything on credit — washers, fridges, the lot, whereas we always saved up till we could buy them outright. They are also in and out of each other's houses all the time. I couldn't do that — I want to live in my house not anyone else's.

☐   I'm in the first generation to buy property in our family. My mother said,

"Buy and be different to us. We've paid to the council for this house over and over again." So when I was nineteen I started saving with the Halifax. The trouble was, in those days you could only get 70% mortgages. They wanted us to buy new, badly built property and discouraged us from doing up this old cottage. My husband worked all the hours God sent, he did two jobs, a job to feed us and another to make the deposit — but he could never reach the magic figure; that despite having put money into the building society.

In the end we approached the council. They were much more understanding. We took out a council mortgage.

☐   A lot of people wouldn't know how to buy, the legal stuff would put the fear of God in them. I see a house as somewhere to live. In our previous, army accommodation there were strict rules — no wallpaper, paint only in regulation colours — this is different, it's mine.

*Queens Terrace double deckers*

*High rise*

*St. John's Church Ladies' Cricket, West Vale*

☐ You need to own more than the house. It's the land you need. Ownership of land is a big plus when it comes to developing ideas on what you think your home should look like. A lot of people waste their imaginations on trying to improve the look of a few square yards of terraced house front. Stone cladding must be the curse of the 1980s although that is mainly to do with the limited amount people are allowed to own. When people get their hands on the land, instead of a few bricks and mortar, then we'll see more imagination.

☐ Owning a house gives young people the privacy they need when they become adults. Privacy is one of the most appealing sides of house ownership to me. For the same reasons, I wouldn't choose a house near the shops or a roadside and I certainly wouldn't want to share with anyone. Living in a communal environment might be alright for economic reasons but it's hardly any different to living with your parents. I wouldn't want the responsibility of living in a house where I had to please other people all the time. I suppose my dream home would be somewhere in the countryside outside of Halifax where I could please myself, not totally remote but far enough away for privacy.

☐ I can't afford to buy. I rent an underdwelling — do you know what that is? Where there's a house built on a steep hill you convert the extra bit below into a separate one-up one-down. They're all homes if you live in them.

☐ I'm happy living with my mum and dad and as I'm twenty now I can see that my taste might change. The only houses I wouldn't want to live in are those with red bricks. I can't stand the colour. I'd really like a bungalow somewhere comfy.

☐ I've lived in a bungalow for 19 years, nearly all my life. I'm happy living at home — most of my friends do except one or two who've got married. I suppose if I meet somebody I would move. I'd prefer to get a bungalow — I can't imagine lugging my vacuum cleaner upstairs.

☐ I shared a house with two other girls when I was a student. It's okay as long as you have a strict rota of work, cooking, cleaning and so on, and as long as everybody pays their share on time. It's usually money and untidiness that causes the rows when you're sharing.

☐ I'm 17 and still with my parents, but I'm working and saving for my first house. I'll try to get a mortgage on a small property, do it up and move on to something a bit better. A house gives you access to a better standard of living. There's no getting away from that kind of chain — the idea of buying and selling already exists, so you're forced to take part in it, if you want to get on in life. It's the same with council house tenants as far as I can see. Most of them will jump at the chance to get a foot on the first rung of the ladder. It seems to help people to look after their homes better as well. If you own a car, you don't want anybody kicking the doors and you don't thrash the gear box, like you would if it was only a company car.

☐ When we first got married we rented a back-to-back house up Commercial Road. It was a one-up one-down with a little box room, an attic and cellar. The rent was 7/6 a week and we paid 7/6 on furniture that we'd got from Rayner's shop on Princess Arcade. We had a three piece moquette suite, it wasn't dear, about £26. We also got a long table for baking on, a square table and four chairs for meals, a black and chrome fender companion set, a cheap carpet — but it did — with oilcloth round, and oilcloth upstairs. For buying there the shop gave us a gift of half a dozen teaspoons.

*Crown Street 1886*

73

Before we got married we went down Crossley Street and put half a crown a week on a card. Out of that we were able to buy a complete dinner service, tea cups, knives, forks, tin opener and a set of fruit dishes. My first fitted carpet was a Wilton that cost £20 at Dean Clough. My husband worked there and had so much a week stopped off his wage. It lasted forty years and went in three houses did that carpet.

We used to dry the washing in the attic and then when my daughter was born she had it as a bedroom. We had a tin bath in the cellar and a gas boiler to fill it. I used to bathe the little girl and then my husband would get into the same water.

After everything was sorted in our first house and the furniture was in, I waved my husband off to work one day and sat down and had a look round. I was the happiest woman in the world and we had it all to pay for. Now my dream home is a cottage on Stretchgate Lane, Pellon.

☐  I lived in my first house over forty years. It was a back-to-back one-up one-down with a little kitchen, up Savile Park. We paid thirty shillings a month when we first moved there but we bought all our furniture second hand. We had a moquette suite, sideboard with mirror, table and four chairs and a carpet square. We had patterned oil cloth everywhere else. The only furniture we had upstairs was a bed and some bit rugs that I had made.

☐  When we first married we lived in a back-to-back in Sowerby Bridge which cost half a crown a week and had a sink in a cupboard. We got the furniture from Jays near Halifax Bus Station. There was a moquette suite, a table and four chairs, a pair of drawers, a bed and a wardrobe. I think we paid two shillings a week and they gave us a mirror free. I've still got that mirror; it's beautiful, all coloured glass, everybody admires it.

After that we got our dream home, a show house in Sowerby Bridge against the church; a semi-detached with front room, kitchen, two bedrooms and a bathroom. It cost £355. To secure it we put £5 down and paid ten shillings a week. To furnish it Mother gave us a piano, we bought a new bedroom suite, which I still have today, and we got some carpets cheap from Humphrey's because my husband worked there I had a good job as well, which helped out a lot. I was a spinner at Lees' Cotton Mill on 39/11d a week.

We sold that house for over a thousand pounds, bought and sold a few more and then decided to move to the countryside for my son's health. We took a cottage on the hilltops outside Sowerby. It was one of a row of five and cost 1/6d a week rent. We put all the money we had made on buying and selling in the bank.

☐  I live in a converted pub. The old beer cellars are great for storage space and the central heating system. The lounge is where the pub's bar was and we kept the old pub name for the house name. We're up on the hills outside Halifax, a beautiful place really, no problems with vandalism, but a prime spot for burglars. Most of the houses nearby have alarms fitted or guard dogs.

☐  I was born in Barkisland in a cottage that was one of a row of three. We walked nearly two miles to school and came home for dinner.

We had just one room downstairs, no kitchen, two bedrooms, and a little entrance hall where we got washed in a bowl on a table. We had no gas, electricity or running water. Light came from an oil lamp hung from the ceiling and we had candles in the bedrooms. We got water from a pump outside the front door.

☐  I was a spinner and got married in 1945. My husband was in the navy. The telegram came on Thursday and we were married on Monday. We had next to nothing compared with what they have now. No fridge, no fitted carpets, just lino.

My ring was a utility one, it is specially marked and cost 29/9d.

The house my daughter lives in now we bought in 1954 before we went down south to make our fortune. It cost us £950, it cost her £24,000.

☐ Few people we knew well owned houses in 1946 although we had an uncle who owned a number. At that time it was a choice between buying a lot of second hand furniture, remember for new furniture you needed dockets, or putting down a deposit on a house and filling it gradually. We chose the house and got one which cost £600. For that we got three bedrooms, a lounge, a kitchen and outside lavatory. This uncle said, "My advice is, buy two — one pays for the other." We had to tell him, "We can only just afford one."

☐ We were thinking of buying a house in Greetland after we got married in 1966. It was £2,200 but we thought who wants to go into debt for £2000? It seemed to us it was either buy your furniture and move into a council house or go into debt and scrimp and save for a comfortable home. We moved away to Lincolnshire in 1969 and only came back here in 1981. Those houses in Greetland are selling for £60,000 to £70,000 now.

☐ We got our first house when we were newly married. We saved two years for the deposit and we only got it after a lot of looking. We bought it because of the position, a terraced cottage in the countryside. We've moved once since, somewhere bigger, a lodgegate house. It was much harder moving because you've to go in one day as such. I was worried about being so far out. It's two miles to the bus stop but I love the countryside. We had to stop this morning for a duck and seven ducklings on the road. It took me twelve months to settle; gradually it becomes home. I suppose it's doing what we want to do to it that makes the

*Union Street, Halifax c. 1925*

*South Place, Wards End 1910*

difference. My favourite room is the lounge — that's the only one we've finished. The rest are all plasterboard. It's hard going. We have to decorate at night when the kids are in bed. We don't do so many nights. We're on a fixed rate mortgage so it only changes yearly — but you dread the next year.

☐   We bought a cottage, it was cheaper than renting a council house. There was always an alternative in cheap housing in Elland up to a few years ago. I think council houses are too dear now and all the better council housing is getting sold off. People who have been trying to make money out of buying and selling council houses have got their fingers burned. The value of the property has not been realised because of where the house is. I can't say that I feel sorry for them.

We have seen some really nice small developments in Bradford that have been built recently. Some of the small

developments for older people with wardens show what can be done.

## Safer with the professionals?

☐   I'm a house agent and I'll tell you this, we hate gazumping. We prefer it to be simple: advertising plus 1%. If someone gazumps, say, an extra £1,000, by law you have to report it to the vendor and, quite frankly, the hassle isn't worth it.

☐   It's hard to see how young people with massive mortgages sleep at night. My granddaughter and her husband have a mortgage of £65,000. Both of them are working but her salary is only £10,000. They have to repay £450 a month.

☐   I learned my lesson about interest payments the hard way. When I was sixteen, well before the war, I used to have to travel from Sutton-in-Craven to Keighley by bus. It seemed logical to buy a bike. You could buy a Raleigh sit up and beg for £4/19/6d in those days but in the window beside this model was a Raleigh Record for £6/16s. I asked the man how much the weekly payments would be and how much I had to pay in deposit. He said that if I let him have 3/9d I could ride it away. Every week I cycled to the shop with a little book and had the money ticked off. On the last day I said, 'That's it then.''

"Oh no, it's not," he said, "now there's the interest, £1/16s.''

That taught me a lesson. Never again.

The next thing I wanted from there was a radio. "How much this time?" I asked. He gave me the window price. "I want 10% off for cash," I said, and I got it.

☐ I worked in a builder's offices when houses were being built in 1936. These were Bradford figures but it wouldn't be so different from over here. A brickie got £3/7/6d a week and a labourer £2/2s. The houses they were building cost £395, of which the deposit was £5.

☐ I bought my first house in 1941, a through-terrace for £310. They were asking £350 but I beat them down for cash. The conveyancing cost £7 10s. In 1947 I sold for £575, bought a small semi for £925 but kept the mortgage as low as possible. I know what the mortgage interest rate was in 1939, it was 4%. Now it's in the region of 11.75%.

☐ People blindly follow what the estate agents and solicitors say. I think folk take in good faith what they say because of their image as professionals. Anybody can do their own conveyancing. You can buy a book in W.H.Smiths today that tells you how to do it. We are the owners of the properties, not them. It is us who should be controlling the buying, selling and pricing, not them.

*Brighouse ornamentation*

Estate agents and solicitors have certainly exploited their monopoly position. I know some solicitors and they have told me that their highly paid conveyancing work subsidises their less remunerative courtroom work — a very cynical way to justify their behaviour. I think building societies on the whole and especially the big ones have also played an irresponsible role in getting houses to the masses. They allowed more access to greater amounts of money, which in turn causes property to go up and put property out of reach of the very people they were originally trying to encourage.

My brother tried to sell his house without consulting an estate agent. He only had three people interested in the first few months and they didn't pursue it. As soon as he put the proper estate agents' sign up, twenty people came in the same week for a house that was now on offer at a higher price. People think that they are safer with the professionals so even if you are selling something that you own, you don't have the power. Power has been taken away from ordinary folk in the house market, not given to them.

□   We had the deposit on our first house paid as a wedding present. We moved second time into Halifax and third time into a bigger house. Our house we sold to my mum; she paid cash so it was the other end we were waiting for. I've never dealt with estate agents. I've always sold our own house.

I like my house but I'm not fanatical over it. We had a new kitchen put in, my husband put in a new bathroom and I do decorating. We're doing it room by room, money by money. My favourite room is the dining room. It's got French windows out on to the patio and it always has the sun on it.

The lawyers seem to take forever. If you ring up they give you the impression they think you're always moaning. If you don't ring up you don't find out what's happening. I don't know what goes on in the background but they don't seem to earn their money, not that I can see. And they charge for every stamp and every piece of paper. We waited and waited. Then, all within a week, it came to a head and we were off.

We're lucky we started on a mortgage when we did. Our last house we paid mostly cash. Starting out now we'd not be able to afford a one-bedroomed flat. A house is as good as money in the bank, isn't it?

□   I did my own legal work to buy the house. All the solicitors tried to put me off, of course, but it's not difficult. Anyone with 5 O-levels could do it. It's a bit of a worry, you're carrying the can and there's a lot of capital tied up in a house, but it's not a lot of work. Anyone who's done clerical work in an office could manage it. They talk of housing booms, well of course there's a boom — every time house prices go up, solicitors' salaries go up or so it seems.

I got an old ambulance, I saved it from a busyard and we made three trips from London to move.

The house is more like an office at the moment as I'm the Green candidate in the Euro elections. The garden is very important to us. It's not big enough to grow a lot but it's large enough to have green space all round.

## A place to commute from

□   Soon Calderdale will be like Norfolk; newly-marrieds will be living in a caravan in their parents' garden, house prices are going up so quickly. It's all this commuting. It's not reached here quite like it has in other districts, although a lot of people travel daily to Manchester, but I know a man in York who travels daily from York to London. He works on the train going down and reckons it takes less time than it does travelling by car from Kent.

☐ There's a lot of commuters in Hebden Bridge. They've moved here recently. We call them the Granada brigade because a lot of them seem to work for the TV company. They live in their converted barns and travel to Manchester every day.

☐ The train which goes from Doncaster to London takes an hour and a half. That's why, although we are an hour's drive from Doncaster, people have started buying houses up here and the prices have rocketed. It's £4,000 a year to travel first class on the train. That's more than some people are earning in a year here.

## Council housing with a community feel

☐ There will always be a place for council housing but not the type that they are building now. Council housing in the past was built with a community feel about it and related to social considerations.

Now the houses aren't built up around industry, just on land allotted for building, in the hope that industry will follow.

☐ Selling off council houses is all well and good for the people who are established in them already. But financial pressures on young couples are too great and houses have to be provided for them. You need two wages to buy a house but there isn't the necessary back-up for working mothers. They're closing nurseries all the time. Our mothers could stop at home to look after babies because of council houses; we cannot.

☐ It makes me laugh — everybody wants a dream home in the countryside. I'm quite happy with my council house in Mixenden, always have been. This selling off of council houses is nonsense. Buy your own council house and you're trapped forever. You can't sell it because nobody wants to buy somebody else's council house. Even if you do sell it,

*Market Street, Halifax*

79

*Stanley Court, off Queens Road, Halifax 1989*

you've still got to have somewhere else to live.

☐ I know of one man in a coal board house who had an emergency repair. The house had been sold to a private landlord. He went to the phone box and rang the number in London to be told the landlord was in Marbella. He loaded up with 50p coins and went back to the phone box. When he finally managed to get through he was asked to hang on a minute.

☐ My council house was built in the 1950s and I paid £1/2/9d rent. They knocked my old house down, but I had no reservations about moving. I thought my council house was great. Proper kitchen, bathroom, separate toilet.

You have to trust your luck with neighbours but you can just as easily get a bad set on a private estate.

I suppose I would have bought my council house but I'm too old now. Selling

them is alright but they should build a new one for every one they sell.

They're a bit slow with repairs but I can't grumble. I think there's a case for mixing private and council — it might improve the environment. Some don't look after them but home is what you make it.

☐ I've been with the council for 46 years and I wouldn't want to change. I live in a maisonette now. Houses are what you make them, some are like palaces, others are like slums.

These are marvellous houses and I don't agree with selling them. People can go and complain to the council, you can't when somebody else owns the house.

Private house people put their noses down at council tenants. They should mix council with private, that would stop them.

☐ The present Government just aren't doing a great deal for council tenants.

People having to live off the State are getting a raw deal.

## People before pound notes

□    Alderman Gilbert Lawson was Chairman of the Housing Committee and I would say he knew every council house built in Brighouse. He ate, slept and breathed houses. People round here have a lot to thank him for.

□    The most frightening thing is that we're now housing five homeless families a week. Our waiting list is 6300. It's never been so high.

The right to buy is fine for people who aspire to own their own home and can afford to purchase. The problem is that the local authority is not allowed to replace its stock. We used to improve 400-500 homes every year. We had a target of building 100 new houses every year; we never quite reached it. Last year we built six. This year we are building none.

In 1979 7.2m of the borrowing appropriation went on housing plus we had 50% of capital receipts. That's just under 14m in today's price terms. This year we've got 2.3m. That's an 80% cut.

When we sell a council house it goes for £18,000; after discount we end up with about £10,000. In London now they'll sell for £100,000 and the council gets £70,80,90,000. In London they're all panicking because the property market is going down. Here it is still going up. It's all part of the North/South divide. People are moving north to get better houses, and commuting. But that doesn't solve Calderdale's housing problems. The Government believes the private sector will fill the gap but there's no take up in this area by private landlords and Housing Associations will have to borrow capital privately. With interest rates going through the roof, guess who pays for the cost of that borrowing? Tenants — their rents go up and who pays that? 65% of tenants in this area get Housing Benefit. There have been seven cuts in Housing Benefit since 1979. The result is a lot more homeless people.

The scale of the loss of homes to private ownership needs a multi-programmed approach. Why squeeze someone with a proud record? We offer a choice, flexibility, value for money and, most importantly, we're accountable. The cynic in me says the Government puts pound notes before people. The local authority has always put people before pound notes.

Another area of concern is that improvement grants are going to be means tested. I think that's a mistake. Unless people get some inducement they won't repair their houses. They'll put up with a leaking fall pipe without realising it's washing out the joints underneath.

We have to pay a price for any move we make. Abbey Park is an estate built on the Radburn system, like many local authority estates in the sixties and seventies. That's very dense housing with access roads into the estate from various parts and no through roads. If you have a heart attack on Abbey Park you'll be dead before the ambulance can find you. The local authority put forward an improvement scheme to open up through roads, deal with roof problems and windows, even change the depressing colour to something more in keeping with the natural environment. The price we've paid is that a large part of the site has been cleared and sold to Barratts. They have a government grant to build 75 houses. There are strings attached to everything we want to do.

Mr Waldegrave thinks I'm wrong. I think he's wrong. He wrote to me telling me I'm wrong. I've got the letter on the wall. One of these days I'll write back and tell him I've been proved right.

The Government wants to erode the public sector further. No one says that council housing is all sweetness and light, but warts and all, we're local,

*Furnishing Warehouse, Russell Street*

approachable and accountable. There's an emergency service always available. We're committed to doing our best for the community we serve; when we produce our balance sheet, at the end of the day if there is any "profit" — and it's not profit really — we put it back into the service. We're handling tenants' money for their benefit not to produce profit for someone else.

Do you remember *Cathy Come Home*? That was in 1965 and it provoked an outcry. Now the situation is five times worse. I can show you statistics proving that for every one homeless family in 1965 there are 17 now. But where is the outcry this time? Many people are better off. There's no question that housing standards have improved. My parents live in a rented house, my grandparents lived in a two-up two-down. If my grandparents could see my house now they'd think that I had robbed the Bank of England to afford it. Society should be more caring for those who haven't got good accommodation.

☐ The Government has got itself into a series of contradictions. For the last twenty years or more the Conservatives have been pushing the idea that you are somehow socially inadequate if you do not own your own house. England had to become a property owning democracy. Well, when they had sold off and drained the market with their tenants' right to buy policy they recognised that they needed a new idea. What we are seeing now is the attempt to bring in the private landlord. This is a movement away from their previously held position. Private landlords are okay and you are acceptable if you rent from individuals or companies. The real bottom of the pile, according to their new philosophy, are those who rent from the council.

*Maurice Jagger at the Piece Hall*

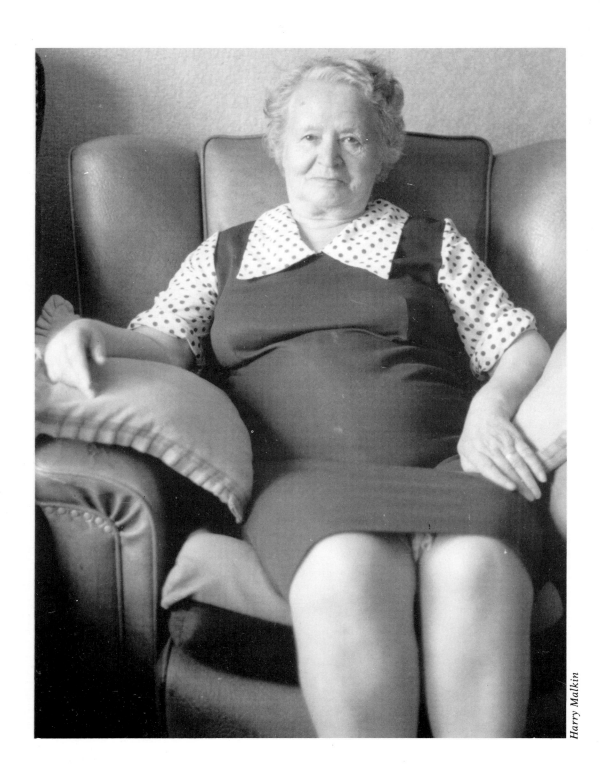

*Harry Malkin*

*All I need is a room somewhere*
*Far away from the cold night air*
*With one enormous chair*
*O wouldn't it be lovely!*

Lerner and Loewe

# HEROES WHO FIT OUT HOMES

*What Makes A House A Home*

## All artex and arches

☐ When we moved into our council house somebody had knocked the wall down between the kitchen and outhouse to make a bigger kitchen. I've fitted a brand new kitchen units with wooden worktops and plenty of cupboard space. I made some mock oak beams with artex and painted them brown, knots in and everything, we trail plants across. I got some wood, stained it to make it look old, and put that on the walls.

I painted the switches and electric points gold but the paint must have reacted with the wiring because I got blue sparks, so I took it off again.

I painted the outside bright red but when the council came they burned it off and painted it cream.

I've had all sorts in the garden, turf, a rockery, and a goldfish pond with gnomes but now I've just got it gravelled.

Our bathroom is in Victoria plum, all fitted. We've a coal fire in the kitchen. I built the fireplace myself from stone I found on a tip. In the front room we have an electric fire, but I built a red brick surround with a wooden varnished mantelpiece to set it off.

☐ You know that old saying "never go by appearances". Take a look at some of those terraced rows and council houses where people bought. Stone cladding only covers up the sins of the house.

☐ You can't impose taste on people as far as decorating their house is concerned. Let them get on with it and call them daft afterwards. The daftest thing I've seen down our street are the people who have ripped out their old windows and put in foul coloured frames, with tacky modern stained glass. It shows a total lack of responsibility for the rest of the neighbourhood, but what can you do?

☐ My daughter bought a former council house. The problem is it looks like a council house. She's now pebbledashed it and put in new windows and a fancy door.

☐ Some people who buy their own houses take it too far, I think. Friends of ours spend all weekend doing DIY and you daren't breathe in their house. They don't go out much any more, just sit there in their Wendy House. It would hurt them more if you criticised their house or car than if you criticised them.

☐ People are becoming totally obsessed with DIY culture. The Sunday morning DIY centres are making a packet out of people with the urge to improve the look of their house, mainly with fixtures and fittings like mock gold bathroom taps and slatted kitchen swing doors. I'm sure they wouldn't buy if it wasn't thrown at them.

☐ When we first went into the house it was a dump but I did it all up with that wooden panelling. I also knocked the cubby hole out to make the kitchen bigger. You should not do that in a council house but I didn't stay around long enough to find out what the council would think.

☐ I tell my daughter, "Don't be so houseproud." A fine house don't make me a home. You can have all your mod cons — there's more to life than polishing the sideboard.

☐ Of course the price of things determines what you have in the house. When I was first married, everything had to be new. It was all woodchip and wall panels in those days. At eighteen I wanted

*Temperance Street Church Bobby Dazzlers 1920*

things to be like everyone else's. Copper kettles, horse brasses, that sort of thing, but now I want things to be more individual and to get that I am prepared to wait a bit longer.

□ My record collection makes any place my home. Our present house is all artexed and painted white. The living room has panelling and a stone fireplace. When we bought our furniture we made sure that the colours co-ordinated.

□ I came from a family where you don't get things on the never-never but you wait until you have the money. My mother is the same. I save all my silver coins in little bags and the copper ones in a jar. Even when I get things from a catalogue I always pay straight out. I know catalogue prices are higher than in the shops but if you have a little child it's more convenient to do it that way than to trail all around Halifax.

Now I find myself looking at the way things are made and thinking about the materials. I wouldn't have done that years ago but now with all this talk about fire risks I am prepared to pay a bit more.

## A gorilla in the hallway

□ One of the ways people get ornaments for the house is through death. A relative dies and the son or daughter brings an ornament round saying, "Mom always said that you admired this so we thought that you would like it." Even if you couldn't remember having seen it before, it has to go up on the shelf.

The things your children bring back from the seaside need to go on view at least for a while.

□ The strangest thing I have ever seen in a house is a wishing well; a bus driver and his wife had one. I've also seen strange pets. Snakes are off putting; they get fed on worms. I could have coped with the frogs if the woman hadn't insisted on showing me the stick insects she fed to them. The biggest frog, a massive coloured thing, was fed on locusts that she kept in a box.

Then there's stuffed animals. My boyfriend's father has a six foot camel which he bought from a window display in Huddersfield. They've also got a gorilla in the hall. Mind, it's a big house.

☐ I chose the paintings in our house. I like something to be well framed but I don't try to match the colours to the curtains. For the picture which is over the fireplace I'll choose rust and beige. Those colours go with everything. I've a picture of a stag at the moment. My husband bought a picture of a sporting dog, done quite well really, which he wanted to put in the alcove but I said, "Over my dead body" and agreed to have it in the hallway. After a few weeks there I took it up into the bedroom and then, when I thought that he wouldn't notice, I put it face down on top of the wardrobe. Gradually I sneak all his things into plastic bags and put them into the loft.

He's always coming home with pool trophies that he has won. I keep them on display for a bit but then pack them away. Once we had a jumble sale so I decided to sell all that stuff. Well, my husband and the little boy came and of course the lad had to say, "You're always winning pool trophies, Dad." My husband then looked carefully and realised that his name was on every one in the collection. He took it well, considering.

☐ We've always done our own decorating, one room at a time. I am houseproud so it's got to be tidy. I go mad on ornaments, especially Hummel figures, they're good quality. My favourite pictures were done in marquetry by my son. I also have a tapestry on my wall which I did myself.

☐ Just before I left school in 1942 our needlework teacher encouraged me to do a small piece of Jacobean style needlework. It was mostly in button-hole stitch but one of the sections I remember was darned, just like you darn a sock. My maiden name was on it, Joan Hudson. There were stylised leaves, trees and an acorn.

It was up on our wall until one of the children broke the frame. I have still got it somewhere but it's very dusty now.

☐ My dream house will grow out of my present bedroom and the houses I have known. My parents' house is a modern one with paper thin walls but my grandfather's is a seventeenth century farm house up on the moors above Owram; I would like something like that.

Since my bedroom is filled with three of my interests — music, history and fantasy art work — my future house will be based on the same things. Like in my present bedroom its contents will gradually grow. There will be history books and articles which are close to my postcard collection.

Now I have pictures from cathedrals; cards of illuminated manuscripts from places like Winchester showing the story of David, a close-up of the hands of creation from Michelangelo's Sistine Chapel painting and a card from Jorvik. In the future I will have tapestries or things I make myself. There will also be personal things. I made my boyfriend climb a wall at Ogden Reservoir to get me a beautiful piece of drift wood. I'll have things like that and my stone collection including the stone from Mount Vesuvius. A room which reflects you is much more important than clothes.

☐ I'm content to stay with my parents. I've got my own room and I can do what I want with it as far as decoration goes. A job is my first priority. I've been out of work since I left school. Then I might consider trying to buy my own place. A scaled down model of my parents' house, with a bit of a garden, would do to start with.

☐   I wish people would make things to hang on their walls, expressions of themselves. They produce lovely things when they are at school, particularly when they are in infants' schools; when they grow older they take their style from supermarket shelves or their neighbours. Then it's all nudes with flowers behind their ears, or charging elephants, or children with big eyes and tears. The picture I can never make out is the one in which the sky is a swan's wings and naked people are standing around looking fit and miserable.

☐   If my husband and I had arguments they would focus on the house. He would say, "If anyone moved, it would have to be you."
I often think of that and wonder, how do people split up all the furniture and ornaments when they separate?

☐   There was a hard drinking, aggressive Irishman with wild red hair. He was not houseproud, his pride and joy was his water wockerwy. He was an excellent gardener even if he couldn't pronounce his rs or wield a duster. The hose pipes pumped merrily through this mini Venice, emerging in beautiful pools and fountains as if it was the Sun King's Palace at Versailles. What all this did to the foundations of Frank's house and his neighbour's, one dreads to think. In among the watery wonders were Frank's gnomes, nymphs and urns with a splendid naked Adonis as the centre piece. This Adonis was frequently the victim of the local vandals, suffering several painful and undignified assaults upon his person. Luckily, he survived and remained the proud guardian of Fwank's water wockerwy.

☐   I don't know how people relax surrounded by discordant colours and patterns which constantly assault their senses. Paisley curtains, coloured floral wallpaper and psychedelic carpets make

*The Crossley and Porter team 1889*

*Ideal Home 1989*

your eyes ache. The house I'm thinking of has a zig-zag striped suite and is crammed to bursting point with knick-knacks and ornaments. When I am there I always feel threatened by the eyes of a colony of foreign dolls and dinky animals. In addition, there are numerous family photos of goo goo babies, awful weddings and Charles and Diana.

☐ The collection of owls came by accident. For some reason she had got two and because of this everyone imagined that she was into owls. That Christmas everyone got her owls. What a collection, there must have been twenty.

☐ We had lots of framed photos all round the room in enormous heavy frames. My parents would point out and name all our relations using these photos. When I wanted money to go to the pictures Dad always said, "There are plenty of pictures here, on the walls."

"But Dad," I would say, "they're not moving." He would say, "I'll soon move them."

☐ What do I hate to see in a house? That's easy: lamp shades with fringes on them, especially tall lamps, that and a lot of seaside souvenirs. Mind, you have to be careful what you say, garden gnomes and ducks which fly up the wall have a habit of coming back into fashion. You also have to remember that someone's bad taste is another's dream of sophistication.

☐ Our first radio was a crystal set. I don't know how it worked but it had two tiny clips. You had to get them in the right position before you could get a note out. Later we went on to something more elaborate, on which we could listen to the old dance bands like Henry Hall. This set was a big affair but we got music out of it. I always wanted to stay up and listen to it but Mother said we had to go to bed. That would be around 1930 when I was at secondary school.

## Bit rugs and oil cloth

☐  My father was a butcher and we lived on Gladstone Road. A lot of business folk lived there then. I was ten when we moved there in 1916 and I lived there till 1976. It had three cellars that house, a washing cellar, a keeping cellar and a coal cellar, two bedrooms and an attic. The floors were stone but we had plenty of bit rugs. Coats were thick then and when they were worn we cut them up to make rugs.

☐  Grandma had Grandad's old red soldier's tunic in a box in the attic. Well, this one night we had got to the point in making the peg rug where we wanted some scarlet material for the centre panel. She went upstairs and brought it down and we cut this beautiful old coat into strips.

☐  People can romanticise about bit rugs now but I'll tell you this, they were very heavy to put over a line to beat and they held the dirt in. They tell me that they are coming back into fashion. Well, let them as wants them have them. Give me a fitted carpet with a pattern any day.

☐  When I was a girl oilcloth was the most common floor covering, and then linoleum. The trouble with oilcloth was its brittleness, it cracked.

People did not think of fitted carpets until the fifties. There was a transitional stage before they got there. They would surround the decorated carpet square with carpet in a plain colour. If red dominated the centre then they would choose red for the edge.

The first designs I saw which came out of Dean Clough were two patterns — *Sultana* and *Banana*. If you opened a door you knew immediately which one it was. In those days, of course, there were plenty of furniture shops close to where you

*Blackleaded range 1889*

lived; not like now when people shop in big warehouses on the edge of the city. In the centre of Halifax there was Leemings in Lister Street, Cousins in Crown Street, and the Co-op — this was a beautiful store — in Horton Street.

## Wallpaper like Tutankhamun's tomb

□  Mrs Barrett always apologised for the mess the house was in, saying that she hadn't got round to tidying up. She also used the excuse that they were redecorating. Then one day I was admitted to the lounge to view the finished result. Pure gold superglypta covered an entire wall onto which the sun shone, streaming in through the wide bay window. The result was electrifying! I half expected to see the mummy of poor Tutankhamun emerge from behind the gleaming chimney breast uttering a curse on us all for desecrating his tomb.

□  We used to have a bar in the corner of the front room with all the bottles and glasses on show. It looked lovely. Mind, we never drank in the house.

□  When I was first married I relied on my husband to do the Do It Yourself jobs while I would do the decorating. As time has gone on I have felt myself more competent. Now I can use a screwdriver and an electric drill. When I start a job and he sees it when he comes home he will sometimes say, "Oh my God, what have you done now?" but really he's not surprised to see me have a go.

□  Wallpapering was something you did not enter into lightly. In the war when there was a paper shortage people made do with distemper which they brightened up with dabs of a different colour damped with a sponge but nowadays they want something different.

My job was to cut the edging from the roll with a pair of scissors. It was a long

*Microwave oven 1989*

91

*The Wood family, Elland c. 1900*

and tedious job. People used edging in a variety of ways. Some placed it at the top of the wallpaper strip where it met the picture rail, others used it so that it touched all pieces of woodwork and some made it into geometrical patterns for a centre piece.

Dad always did the wallpapering.

☐ Although I gave my daughters in the sixties some say in how they decorated their room – they used posters mostly – I was not given much choice. As I got older I was allowed to help choose the wallpaper but that was it really. I could say that my room was my room but it didn't amount to much. You couldn't do much with a chest of drawers, a bed and a mirror. The contrast between the generations has to be seen to be believed. One of my girls, I remember, had three walls light green and the other dark. All that, and designer untidy. I spent a lot of time keeping my room in order.

## Jaffa on the drawers inside

☐ In those days just after the war you needed a docket to get furniture. It was like rationing but for all that, utility furniture was the best there was. It was plain but it was well built. My sister still has the bedroom suite and that's forty five years later. Before the war everything was built to last, not like now when it's all glass and rubbish. Now you can only expect to have a cooker for five years; try to get a part after that and they'll tell you it is obsolete.

☐ We used to swap dockets so we could get what we wanted. A friend of mine had a sideboard and when you took the drawers out, it had Jaffa written on the inside. She had it years. Orange boxes in those days must have been good.

☐ If you stand in the middle of Halifax and look straight down Horton Street you will see a big house half way up Beacon Hill. It has been there for centuries. I say you will see a house but actually it is four houses. I spent my childhood during the Second World War in the bottom storey of that building. We were half way through the twentieth century but I was living a lifestyle which bridged back to Victorian times.

## One pip for twenty pound of apples

☐ I was widowed when my youngest was three so I never had much time to bother with the garden. Ours was no more than a long piece of land with a lawn for the kids to play on.

One of our kids put a seed in a jar, it set off growing till it nearly reached the top of the living room window. We took it outside and planted it near the back window. Soon it was knocking at the window so we had to replant it at the bottom of the garden. After about seven years some white blossom appeared, we realised then it was an apple tree. The kids used to raid it every year. It's still there now, it's been growing above twenty years. They were only crab apples but my lad used to make wine of them. I bet he got twenty pounds off it one year.

☐ I had flowers in the front garden and vegetables at the back; potatoes, cabbage, peas, onions, all the lot. We were able to keep ourselves going with the veg I grew. Nowadays the council put lawns around the flats and houses and their own workers come round to tend them. Nobody bothers growing their own stuff now.

☐ I think these garden centres are marvellous. You can drive there at any time and they've got all sorts. If I had the money, I'd spend a lot of time there but I haven't, so what I do is look around them and pick up tips. I've built my own pond

*Mixenden Church Gardens 1988*

93

*Painting a tepee, Mixenden 1989*

out of plastic sheeting and some broken flagstones I found and a bird table out of scraps of wood. I picked up an old sawn up tree and built a summer table and four chairs out of logs. It gives what they call a rustic effect. Mine is probably the best looking patio on the estate.

☐  Recreation grounds don't seem to exist as I knew them when I was a kid. Now it's all *Keep Off The Grass* wherever you look. There must be a case for creating large grassed play areas in council estates to keep kids off the gardens in front of the houses. What were once lawns are now nothing more than quagmires.

There should be more incentives to keep nice gardens. Garden contests for example, vegetable championships. I've seen some gardens that are a joy to behold but when you go down Mixenden and see in big blue letters on the bus shelter, "Mixy Riot Squad" it puts you off looking for nice gardens.

☐  My husband was in the services and we lived in services housing in Southampton and Ipswich before we moved back up here. I think a lot of tenants don't look after their houses. If it was their own they'd take more care. You can tell by the garden what the house is like. If the garden is neat and tidy then the house will be neat and tidy. It is a happy family atmosphere that makes a home though.

☐  When I was in my teens living in Mixenden the council ran a competition for the best garden. My mother thought we should have a go so we got stuck in and picked up all the litter. We then turned to the weeds and pulled up most of the flowers as well. When it was lawned with roses all round, we whitewashed all the flags. It looked horrible.

☐  It's hard to do any gardening in Mixenden. The earth is hard clay and floods a lot. There's bad design of the dustbin area as well and rubbish blows about all over when the dogs get into the bins.

☐ It's nice to live near a park or somewhere you can take the kids for a walk. All the dog mess is annoying though, especially with kiddies around. They should make people pay more for dog licences.

☐ I have an open plan garden which the council refuse to fence in until 1992 because they want to do a drainage system. So I end up with a garden full of dog dirt, broken bottles and tin cans. My daughter cut her leg falling in the garden. I sued the council for £500 but they still wouldn't put a fence up. After that I collected up all the tin cans and dog shit and dumped it on the floor of the council office and told them that they'd get it every week until they built me a new fence, but I'm still without one.

There is a swing park nearby but bigger kids put tar and paint on the swings so the little ones can't go on there. The swings and see-saws are badly designed on concrete bases. Kids are always falling and hurting themselves.

☐ There was a lovely garden in Sunnybank Road. The old man was moving out and said that if he was going then the garden had to go as well. The council were good about it. All the plants were carefully put into pots and great care was taken with the more mature plants and trees. The council made every effort to look after that garden.

☐ Taste? Who dictates that? If we lived in a free society everybody would have as many gnomes as they wanted in the front garden.

☐ My garden was completely overgrown, it looked like desert weed. I fetched three donkeys to gnaw it all down.

*Dick Taylor of Elland in the breakers yard c. 1910*

95

The farmer lent me them. They did a great job, chewed it right down. The only trouble was, to get them to the back garden we had to take them through the house. There were two females and a male. We took the male through first, tapping him with a stick. He only just fit through the door hole, he had also got a hard-on, then the females followed. It was worse getting them out though, because they were a lot fatter.

After that the whole neighbourhood wanted to use them. They went from house to house. Afterwards there was a complaint to the council. They came round and realised we must have had the donkeys in the house. I kidded them on, telling them, "Some people keep dogs as pets, I keep donkeys."

☐  The person next door to us decided to breed chickens. He had nearly six hundred chickens in his house jumping all over his furniture. He put them into his garden. He used to kill them, pluck them and sell them for a pound apiece. I plucked one for him once but I got lice running up my arm. I got straight into the bath; it was the first and last one I ever plucked. They were good quality chickens.

☐  The council leafleted us to tell us about the Calderdale gardening competition. I won the *Best Garden In a Refurbished House* category two years in succession, 1987 and 1988. I got a special merit award. I suppose it surprised one or two when they found out the winning garden was in Mixenden and I was only in my twenties. I've always been creative, especially with flowers. They look much nicer than vegetables in a garden.

I grow my flowers from seed packets. I used to have cold frames to start them off but they looked a bit ugly so I got shut. To stop dogs getting in I built up my fence from scraps of wood I found about, then I lined the bottom of the fence with broken paving slabs to stop litter blowing in.

I get peat from the woods and manure from the fields. You see, I believe that you have to put back into the earth what you take from it. The soil's not too good round here so I put new soil in as well. Latest additions have been an ornamented well with a pond, rustic fencing and a bird house. I saw a bird house in town for £30. I couldn't afford it so I built one myself, a much better one, it's like a tiered wedding cake.

I get things pinched from my garden but it doesn't dishearten me. It's all worth it when you see a nice display of flowers.

☐  You don't know your neighbour now. He might be a commuter. Privacy is a commodity for rich people but I would not want it. I have a social investment in my community and like to know I can call on my neighbours if I want. A house is the haven of a family, the neighbourhood is the harbour and then it is the open world. If you don't have haven and harbour then you are open to all sorts of abuses.